Praise for Michael E. Gerber, Than Merrill, Paul Esajian, and *The E-Myth Real Estate Investor*

Than Merrill is the "ultimate coach" for that special breed of real estate investor who never wants to settle for being less than they can be. I have worked hand in hand with him for years, and he is **always on the cutting edge of helping investors automate their real estate businesses.**

Pat Precourt, short sale expert

Than Merrill is the leading teacher and coach in the real estate investment industry. Not only will *The E-Myth Real Estate Investor* change the way you think about your real estate business, but Than's warmth, commitment, and passion will **inspire you to truly master your business and improve your life.**

Cort Christie, CEO and founder, Nevada Corporate Headquarters

If you are looking to own your business instead of having your business own you, then you have to read *The E-Myth Real Estate Investor* **by Than Merrill.** I have met countless real estate investors over the years who now have very successful real estate businesses because of Than's guidance and coaching.

Greg Clement, founder, Realeflow.com

The E-Myth Real Estate Investor **should be required reading for every real estate entrepreneur.** No one has positively impacted more real estate investors' businesses and lives than Than Merrill.

Sean Malarkey, blogger and author

Michael Gerber's *The E-Myth* is one of only four books I recommend as required reading. **For those looking to start and build a business of their own, this is the man who has coached more successful entrepreneurs than the next ten gurus combined.**

Timothy Ferris, #1 *New York Times* best-selling author, *The 4-Hour Workweek*

Everyone needs a mentor, someone who tells it like it is, holds you accountable, and shows you your good, bad, and ugly. For millions of small-business owners, Michael Gerber is that person. Let Michael be your mentor and you are in for a kick in the pants, the ride of a lifetime.

John Jantsch, author, *Duct Tape Marketing*

Michael Gerber's strategies in *The E-Myth* were instrumental in building my company from two employees to a global organization; I can't wait to see how applying the strategies from *Awakening the Entrepreneur Within* will affect its growth!

Dr. Ivan Misner, founder and chairman, BNI; author, *Masters of Sales*

Michael Gerber's gift to isolate the issues and present simple, direct, business-changing solutions shines bright with *Awakening the Entrepreneur Within*. **If you're interested in developing an entrepreneurial vision and plan that inspires others to action, buy this book, read it, and apply the processes Gerber brilliantly defines.**

Tim Templeton, author, *The Referral of a Lifetime*

Michael Gerber is a master instructor and a leader's leader. As a combat F-15 fighter pilot, I had to navigate complex missions with life-and-death consequences, but until I read *The E-Myth* and met Michael Gerber, my transition to the world of small business was a nightmare with no real flight plan. **The hands-on, practical magic of Michael's turnkey systems magnified by the raw power of his keen insight and wisdom have changed my life forever.**

Steve Olds, CEO, Stratworx.com

Michael Gerber truly, truly understands what it takes to be a successful practicing entrepreneur and business owner. He has demonstrated to me over six years of working with him that for those who stay the course and learn much more than just "how to work on their business and not in it," then they will reap rich rewards. **I finally franchised my business, and the key to unlocking this kind of potential in any business is the teaching of Michael's work.**

Chris Owen, marketing director, Royal Armouries (International) PLC

Michael's work has been an inspiration to us. **His books have helped us get free from the out-of-control life that we once had. His no-nonsense approach kept us focused on our ultimate aim rather than day-to-day stresses. He has helped take our business to levels we couldn't have imagined possible.** In the Dreaming Room™ made us totally re-evaluate how we thought about our business and our life. We have now redesigned our life so we can manifest the dreams we unearthed in Michael's Dreaming Room™.

Jo and Steve Davison, founders, The Spinal Health Clinic
Chiropractic Group and www.your-dream-life.com

Because of Michael Gerber, I transformed my twenty-four-hour-a-day, seven-day-a-week job (also called a small business) into a multimillion-dollar turnkey business. This in turn set the foundation for my worldwide training firm. **I am living my dream because of Michael Gerber.**

Howard Partridge, Phenomenal Products Inc.

Michael Gerber is an outrageous revolutionary who is changing the way the world does business. **He dares you to commit to your grandest dreams and then shows you how to make the impossible a reality. If you let him, this man will change your life.**

Fiona Fallon, founder, Divine and The Bottom Line

Michael Gerber is a genius. Every successful business person I meet has read Michael Gerber, refers to Michael Gerber, and lives by his words. You just can't get enough of Michael Gerber. **He has the innate (and rare) ability to tap into one's soul, look deeply, and tell you what you need to hear. And then, he inspires you and equips you with the tools to get it done.**

Pauline O'Malley, CEO, TheRevenueBuilder

When asked "Who was the most influential person in your life?" I am one of the thousands who don't hesitate to say "Michael E. Gerber." **Michael helped transform me from someone dreaming of retirement to someone dreaming of working until age one hundred.** This awakening is the predictable outcome of anyone reading Michael's new book.

Thomas O. Bardeen

Michael Gerber is an incredible business philosopher, guru, perhaps even a seer. He has an amazing intuition, which allows him to see in an instant what everybody else is missing; he sees opportunity everywhere. **While I was in the Dreaming Room™, Michael gave me the gift of seeing through the eyes of an awakened entrepreneur, and instantly my business changed from a regional success to serving clients on four continents.**

Keith G. Schiehl, president, Rent-a-Geek Computer Services

Michael Gerber is among the very few who truly understand entrepreneurship and small business. While others talk about these topics in the form of theories, methodologies, processes, and so on, Michael goes to the heart of the issues. **Whenever Michael writes about entrepreneurship, soak it in, as it is not only good for your business, but great for your soul.** His words will help you to keep your passion and balance while sailing through the uncertain sea of entrepreneurship.

Raymond Yeh, co-author, *The Art of Business*

Michael Gerber forced me to think big, think real, and gave me the support network to make it happen. A new wave of entrepreneurs is rising, much in thanks to his amazing efforts and very practical approach to doing business.

Christian Kessner, founder, Higher Ground Retreats and Events

Michael's understanding of entrepreneurship and small-business management has been a difference maker for countless businesses, including Infusion Software. **His insights into the entrepreneurial process of building a business are a must-read for every small-business owner.** The vision, clarity, and leadership that came out of our Dreaming Room™ experience were just what our company needed to recognize our potential and motivate the whole company to achieve it.

Clate Mask, president and CEO, Infusion Software

Michael Gerber is a truly remarkable man. His steady openness of mind and ability to get to the deeper level continue to be an inspiration and encouragement to me. **He seems to always ask that one question that forces the new perspective to break open, and he approaches the new coming method in a fearless way.**

Rabbi Levi Cunin, Chabad of Malibu

The Dreaming Room™ experience was literally life-changing for us. **Within months, we were able to start our foundation and make several television appearances owing to his teachings.** He has an incredible charisma, which is priceless, but above all Michael Gerber awakens passion from within, enabling you to take action with dramatic results . . . starting today!

Shona and Shaun Carcary
Trinity Property Investments Inc. — Home Vestors franchises

I thought *E-Myth* was an awkward name! What could this book do for me? **But when I finally got to reading it . . . it was what I was looking for all along.** Then, to top it off, I took a twenty-seven-hour trip to San Diego just to attend the Dreaming Room™, where Michael touched my heart, my mind, and my soul.

Helmi Natto, president, Eye 2 Eye Optics, Saudi Arabia

I attended In the Dreaming Room™ and was challenged by Michael Gerber to "Go out and do what's impossible." So I did; **I became an author and international speaker and used Michael's principles to create a world-class company that will change and save lives all over the world.**

Dr. Don Kennedy, MBA; author, *5 AM & Already Behind*, www.bahbits.com

I went to the Dreaming Room™ to have Michael Gerber fix my business. He talked about Dreaming. What was this Dreaming? I was too busy working! Too busy being miserable, angry, frustrated, behind in what I was trying to accomplish. And losing everything I was working for. **Then Michael Gerber woke up the dreamer in me and remade my life and my business.**

Pat Doorn, president, Mountain View Electric Ltd.

Michael Gerber can captivate a room full of entrepreneurs and take them to a place where they can focus on the essentials that are the underpinning of every successful business. He gently leads them from where they are to where they need to be in order to change the world.

Francine Hardaway, CEO, Stealthmode Partners
founder, the Arizona Entrepreneurship Conferences

The E Myth

Real Estate Investor

*Why Most Real Estate Investment
Businesses Don't Work
and What to Do About It*

MICHAEL E. GERBER
THAN MERRILL
and PAUL ESAJIAN

PRODIGY
BUSINESS BOOKS

Published by
Prodigy Business Books, Inc., Carlsbad, California.

Production Team
Patricia Beaulieu, COO, Prodigy Business Books, Inc.; Helen Chang, editor,
AuthorBridgeMedia.com; Erich Broesel, cover designer, BroeselDesign, Inc.;
Nancy Ratkiewich, book production, njr productions; Jeff Kassebaum, Michael
E. Gerber author photographer, Jeff Kassebaum and Co.; Than Merrill co-author
photographer, Cindy Phillips; Paul Esajian co-author photographer, David Lupica

For general information on other products and services, please visit the website:
www.michaelegerber.com.

ISBN 978-0-98355-426-4 (cloth)
ISBN 978-1-61835-004-6 (audio)

Printed in the United States of America

10 9 8 7 6 5 4 3 2 1

To Luz Delia, whose heart expands mine,
whose soul inspires mine,
whose boldness reaches for the stars, thank you,
forever, for being, truly mine . . .

—Michael E. Gerber

CONTENTS

A WORD ABOUT THIS BOOK

Michael E. Gerber

My first E-Myth book was published in 1985. It was called *The E-Myth: Why Most Small Businesses Don't Work and What to Do About It*. Since that book, and the company I created to provide business development services to its many readers, millions have read *The E-Myth*, and the book that followed it called *The E-Myth Revisited*, and tens of thousands have participated in our E-Myth Mastery programs.

One of the co-authors of this book, Than Merrill, is one of my more enthusiastic readers, and as a direct result of his enthusiasm, his real estate investment company became one of those clients. He became, over the years, one of my friends.

This book is two things: the product of my lifelong work conceiving, developing, and growing the E-Myth way into a business model that has been applied to every imaginable kind of company in the world, as well as a product of Than's extraordinary experience and success applying the E-Myth to the development of his equally extraordinary enterprise, FortuneBuilders Inc.

So it was that one day, while sitting with my muse, which I think of as my inner voice, and which many who know me think of as "here he goes again!" I thought about the creation of an entire series of E-Myth Expert books. That series, including this book, would be co-authored by experts in every industry who had successfully applied my E-Myth principles to the extreme development of a sole proprietorship—an employer plus one—with the intent of growing it nationwide, and even worldwide, which is what Than had in mind as he began to discover the almost infinite range of opportunities provided by thinking the E-Myth way.

Upon seeing the possibilities of this new idea, I immediately invited co-authors such as Than to join me. They said, "Let's do it!" and so we did.

Welcome to *The E-Myth Real Estate Investor: Why Most Real Estate Investment Businesses Don't Work and What to Do About It.*

Read it, enjoy it, and let us—Than, Paul, and I—help you apply the E-Myth to the re-creation, development, and extreme growth of your real estate investment company into an enterprise that you can be justifiably proud of.

To your life, your wisdom, and the life and success of your clients, I wish you good reading.

—Michael E. Gerber
Co-Founder/Chairman
Michael E. Gerber Companies, Inc.
Carlsbad, California
www.michaelegerber.com/co-author

A NOTE FROM THAN AND PAUL

Than Merrill
Paul Esajian

This book will change you. It will change the way you think, how you act, your approach to work, and, ultimately, it will change your life.

Yes, this is a bold promise. One we intend to keep. The question is: Are you the type of person who is ready for this type of massive change? Or are you the type of person, who, like most people, buy a book, read a chapter or two, and then put it back on the shelf?

Please don't ever put this book on that shelf. This book hates being anywhere near those books. You owe it to yourself and your financial future to read this sleek, sexy book! Well, that's the first step. You will then have to commit to implementing what you learn into your real estate investment business.

Now, let us be frank about what this book is about and what it isn't.

This book will not teach you the mechanics of how to do real estate deals. This book will not teach you everything you need to know about how to analyze a deal. This book will not teach you how to creatively finance a deal, how to raise private money, how to negotiate a purchase and sale agreement, or how to estimate the repair cost of a property.

Yes, these are all very important aspects of the real estate investing business that you must learn and master if you expect to be successful. However, this book is about something much more important than the mechanics of doing real estate deals. It will teach you the philosophy of how a successful business is built, and ultimately it will change the way you think about your own business.

Consider it to be an awakening, and our gift to you and your business.

This book represents the collective efforts and years of business experience of Than and Paul, but for simplicity's sake, the stories in this book are told from Than's viewpoint.

My first entrepreneurial venture was over ten years ago when I started a Mexican restaurant while I was still playing in the NFL for the Chicago Bears. Seriously, what white guy starts a Mexican restaurant while he is still playing in the NFL in the prime of his life? I am not kidding. I distinctly remember warming up before a game against the Minnesota Vikings and getting a call before kickoff from Alfredo, the manager of my restaurant, asking me what to do because we were out of tortillas.

Remember, this was before the E-Myth days.

I started the restaurant because I thought having a good, entre-preneurial idea was enough to make serious money in business. Michael Gerber calls this moment the "entrepreneurial seizure"; well, in my case, it was more of an "entrepreneurial fart."

After injuring my knee and then being released from the NFL (for being too darn fast), I poured all my entrepreneurial energy into the restaurant. I was working twelve- to fourteen-hour days and hating every second of it. Every week we were losing money, and I couldn't figure out how to stop the bleeding no matter how hard I worked or how many hours I put in.

One night I delivered a burrito to a guy who recognized me from college and NFL days. I remember the puzzled look on his face when he said, "Than, why are you delivering burritos?"

There are moments in everyone's life that have the power to spark massive change. Moments that define your future and the path you ultimately choose to take. I remember walking down that guy's dimly lit driveway and getting back into my car. I just sat there, pondering what my life had become, and I broke down in tears. Not living up to the goals I had set for myself in the NFL and then having my entrepreneurial dream turn into a nightmare was too much for me to handle.

It was at this moment that I decided I was going to make a change and get out of the restaurant business. I didn't have a passion for the business and I knew I had to make a change. Not just any change, but a massive change. Life was too short to continue doing something I didn't have the passion for.

So I immediately started reading books about something I had always had a passion for: real estate. I had no prior knowledge, had never taken a class, and had nobody to ask for advice regarding how to invest, but it didn't matter. I knew I could find the answers and people to learn from if I was determined enough.

I devoured books and courses and started attending many different real estate investing seminars. After months of studying, I decided it was time to take action and buy a few properties. But I knew that I had to continue studying the business and never stop learning. Thus began my personal journey into the real estate investing world.

Even though I was still very new to the business, I realized its potential. I subsequently decided to partner with Paul Esajian, one of my good childhood friends, and Konrad Sopielnikow, one of my old football teammates from Yale University.

Hey, isn't being new and not knowing anything the best way to start a business? Then call your friends who don't know anything, either. At least you can all fail together.

To make ends meet, I was still working long hours in my restaurant, wearing what seemed like fifteen different hats at once. In the early morning and on the weekends, I'd put on my real estate hats. There were days I would wake up in the morning and walk through two or three bank-owned properties that smelled like cat urine only to be followed by ten hours of rolling burritos and making guacamole.

After purchasing a few rental properties, we three partners decided it was time to start flipping real estate. Our goal was to flip a few deals and then sell the restaurant, even if we had to take a huge loss. So that's exactly what we did—and it was the best decision of our lives.

But there was a problem. We all were getting a great real estate education by reading books and going to seminars, but we still had no idea how to run a business. The first nine months of our real estate business looked dangerously similar to the months of handling my failed restaurant.

They say when the student is ready, the teacher will appear. Well, my teacher was a five-foot-three Australian bartender who worked at a local bar down the street. This is not a joke. For some reason, she had been given the book *E-Myth Revisited* written by Michael Gerber, the co-author of the book you are reading now.

I stumbled upon *E-Myth Revisited* one morning while I was looking around her apartment for something to read. I read the tag line on the cover "Why Most Small Businesses Don't Work and What to Do About It" and I remember thinking, Hey, that's my business! Little did I know it was a gift from God!

I immediately started reading it, and that's when I had my personal awakening. It was like being born again, in the business sense. I was so moved by it that I jumped in my car, drove straight to the bookstore, and bought copies for both my partners. I have always been a little obsessive-compulsive when I'm inspired by something. The book spoke to me, and after finishing it I realized why my restaurant had failed and why our real estate business was doomed for mediocrity at best if we didn't change our approach.

I literally forced Paul and Konrad to read *The E-Myth* the next day. The following morning we met to discuss what we had learned. We always had our meetings on the balcony of my condo so Konrad could smoke his big cigars. Konrad always likes having his transformational moments intensified by his good friends and nicotine and/or caffeine. It was very clear that the book's central message had spoken to all of us directly. We compared notes and had a remarkably deep and honest conversation about the vision and direction of our business. We shared our personal, financial, and life goals. We also communicated what we expected from each other if we were really going to build something greater than ourselves.

The remarkable thing was how the book inspired us all to change many of our work habits. At the time, we were all technicians working in and responsible for different areas of the business. As we shared ideas, we each realized that the book had spoken to us in different yet similar ways, based on our own business responsibilities. We discussed exactly how we could improve and automate not only our individual roles within the company, but also the business as a whole.

We prioritized what areas of the business we were going to work on first. We realized we couldn't implement everything at once so we had to have a strategic plan for what needed improvement the most. We all agreed that our approach to our day-to-day work had to change if we wanted to create financial freedom and build something greater than ourselves.

Our first task was to begin "working on the business," and not just "working in the business." It was the first major change we had to make in our daily work habits. We realized that our real estate investment business was something bigger and, more importantly, separate from ourselves, a living entity that we could intentionally design, mold, and create.

The second thing we realized was that we needed systems for all areas of the business. More specifically, we had to document many of the business processes that consumed so much of our time every day. We could never outsource or delegate anything to anyone else, because all the knowledge of what to do was in our heads, but not on paper. Not only were we working inefficiently because we didn't have systems to follow, but we also had no ability to leverage other people's time. Much of our day was spent on busywork and activities that didn't directly drive revenue.

These were all monumental shifts we had to make. Basically, we had been working harder and not smarter. We decided that we needed to work more strategically. We needed to focus on freeing our time so the work we put in would maximize our personal highest and best use.

Then we needed to build systems and replace ourselves so other people could step into our shoes and generate revenue. We knew these systems would take longer to develop, but we had to do it if we ever wanted to free ourselves from the daily grind.

Since our introduction to Michael's book, we have developed over the years from having an academic understanding of the E-Myth philosophy to living it day by day.

Adopting the philosophy into the daily framework of our business was like being "born again" in a business sense. It inspired us to be more strategic in the way we worked. Ultimately, it led us to build a very successful and very profitable real estate business that isn't dependent on our time. We have now bought and sold hundreds of properties and made millions of dollars.

The extraordinary thing about the E-Myth philosophy is that it applies to all real estate businesses and all businesses in general. We have adopted this approach in every business we have started over the years and know firsthand how it can be applied to different industries.

We have used the E-Myth principles to build five other highly successful businesses, including one of the largest real estate training companies in the world: FortuneBuilders.com. We are proud that our training and coaching programs have helped thousands of people launch and build successful real estate investment businesses worldwide. Our philosophy is based on applying principles of the E-Myth to other people's businesses. We start with the philosophy, but more importantly we help people implement the systems and processes we created into their own business.

Through our seminars and coaching program, we have changed the lives of thousands of real estate investors by giving them a sound business model to follow. The systems we spent years developing are the ones we have given to the investors we coach. These "franchise-like" systems are why ordinary people—of all ages, backgrounds, and walks of life—are achieving extraordinary results.

Many of the students we have helped build successful businesses have never had any formal business training or schooling. Some never even graduated from high school. But they became successful by adopting our philosophy, as explained in this book, and then having the desire and focus to implement the systems we designed.

As an experienced real estate investor and someone intimately familiar with how investors think, we know that some of you are skeptical at this stage. You might be saying that it's different for you and that this philosophy won't work in your business. After coaching thousands of investors, we have heard every reason why these principles won't work in other situations.

We've heard countless excuses why they won't work in particular cities. We've heard why they won't work for investors who specialize in wholesaling, rehabs, short sales, lease options, or commercial real estate. However, after coaching countless investors, we've seen that this philosophy—coupled with our systems—can work seamlessly in every market and specialty.

To benefit from this book, you have to first clear away all the misconceptions that somehow your situation is different. You have to become an open slate and be ready to accept change. Otherwise, you will forever be stuck in the daily grind of paperwork and processing deals and terms with unrealistic sellers, unmotivated buyers, and tenants.

The key to changing your perspective is to start looking at your business from the outside instead of the inside. Think of yourself as a business consultant and your first job is tackling your own company and the problems and inefficiencies that exist within it. In order to do this, you will have to slow down and stop working so hard. In some instances you will have to take a temporary step backward in order to take a giant leap forward.

There are some people reading this book who haven't started investing yet or are in the beginning phases of getting educated about the business. There are others who invest but don't really consider it a business. Make no mistake about it: from the very first property you buy, it's a business. This book is about business and how you can build a real estate investment business that has a successful life without your involvement and despite your separation from it.

However, this book is not just about making more and more money every year as an investor. Yes, that will be a natural byproduct of learning this philosophy and implementing our systems. This book is about time. This book is about building a business that makes money, makes you proud, and gives you time to enjoy the lifestyle you desire.

At our real estate educational company, FortuneBuilders.com, this concept is called "lifestyle design." Lifestyle design is about creating a business that produces the results you desire and provides you with the time and freedom to live a life others only dream about. It will give you the freedom to do what you want, when you want, with whomever you want. It will give you the freedom to enjoy life's finer pleasures. It will allow you to not just create a business, but leave a legacy.

As real estate investors, we understand the evolution of the dream that started when you picked up your first book or went to your first seminar about investing. We understand how the dream reached a reality after you completed your first deal and deposited that check into your bank account. We remember the excitement you experienced in the start-up phase when everything you worked on was new, creative, and inspiring.

We also remember how it felt when that dream started to fade, and the daily grind and long hours set in. When previously exciting activities began to feel like nothing more than work. We remember this transition from dreamer to worker. We remember thinking that owning my own business felt like nothing more than a glorified job. A job filled with endless paperwork and phone calls. Unfortunately, after many years of working till my fingernails bled, we also understand how the negativity sets in and replaces that dream. In fact, for most real estate investors, that dream seems like a distant and naïve memory. Throw in market conditions and, all of a sudden, that dream can easily become a nightmare.

Everyone knows that investing in real estate can be highly profitable, and because of that the business attracts many opportunity seekers looking to strike it rich. There is no formal schooling process like in other professions, so people are left to learn on their own or from other successful investors.

Success requires that you learn and acquire many different skill sets. Not only do you have to learn and understand the mechanics of how deals get done, how to raise money, how to increase the value of properties, and determine the proper exit strategy, but you also have to learn how to run a business at the same time. Still, just having that knowledge is not enough to succeed. You must learn how to run a successful business, and that's what most real estate books, courses, and seminars hardly ever teach. Learning how to make money by doing a deal is one thing, but learning how to run a business that does profitable deals without your time and presence is another.

In our eyes, financial freedom is only achieved when you learn how to run a business that is not dependent on your time.

So here we are nine short years later, and we have created a business that literally runs itself. We have a team of highly professional individuals who do 95 percent of the daily work for us. Setting up our real estate business in this way has enabled us to start other companies. It allows us to work when we want, and affords us the opportunity to spend that time working creatively. This is what every entrepreneur desires, but few ever achieve.

Setting up our business the right way now affords us the time to coach other real estate investors. This is what we are most passionate about and what we consider to be our true calling. We love helping people set up and launch their own businesses, and then ultimately free themselves of their businesses. It is highly rewarding work when you can help someone else achieve both financial and personal goals. Giving back is also helping us to leave a legacy in the business that has given us so much over the years.

Reading *The E-Myth* was a defining moment in our entrepreneurial lives. We hope this book has the same kind of impact on you, one that is even deeper and more relevant because it applies the E-Myth philosophy to the real estate business.

It will be a hard road. At times it will suck. You will want to quit. There will be days when you will think that selling insurance doesn't look so bad. Don't give in. Don't give up! Trust us. What you learn in this book can change your life.

Enjoy the journey . . .

—Than Merrill and Paul Esajian
Co-Founders
FortuneBuilders.com
San Diego, California

PREFACE

Michael E. Gerber

I am not a real estate investor, though I have helped dozens of real estate investors reinvent their real estate investment companies over the past thirty-five years.

I like to think of myself as a thinker, maybe even a dreamer. Yes, I like to *do* things. But before I jump in and get my hands dirty, I prefer to think through what I'm going to do and figure out the best way to do it. I imagine the impossible, dream big, and then try to figure out how the impossible can become the possible. After that, it's about how to turn the possible into reality.

Over the years, I've made it my business to study how things work and how people work—specifically, how things and people work best together to produce optimum results. That means creating an organization that can do great things and achieve more than any other organization can.

This book is about how to produce the best results as a real-world real estate investor in the development, expansion, and *liberation* of your company. In the process, you will come to understand what the practice of real estate investment—as a *business*—is, and what it isn't. If you keep focusing on what it isn't, you're destined for failure. But if you turn your sights on what it is, the tide will turn.

This book, intentionally small, is about big ideas. The topics we'll be discussing in this book are the very issues that real estate investors face daily in their company. You know what they are: money, management, clients, and many more. My aim is to help you begin the exciting process of totally transforming the way you do business. As such, I'm confident that *The E-Myth Real Estate Investor* could well be the most important book on the practice of real estate investing as a business that you'll ever read.

Unlike other books on the market, my goal is not to tell you how to do the work you do. Instead, I want to share with you the E-Myth philosophy as a way to revolutionize the way you think about the work you do. I'm convinced that this new way of thinking is something real estate investors everywhere must adopt in order for their real estate investment company to flourish during these trying times. I call it strategic thinking, as opposed to tactical thinking.

In strategic thinking, also called systems thinking, you, the real estate investor, will begin to think about your entire company—the broad scope of it—instead of focusing on its individual parts. You will begin to see the end game (perhaps for the first time) rather than just the day-to-day routine that's consuming you—the endless, draining work I call "doing it, doing it, doing it."

Understanding strategic thinking will enable you to create a company that becomes a successful business, with the potential to flourish as an even more successful enterprise. But in order for you to accomplish this, your company, your business, and certainly your enterprise must work *apart* from you instead of *because* of you.

The E-Myth philosophy defines a company as a sole proprietorship, a business, or an enterprise, so you will see these designations used throughout the book. In some industries, a company can also be called a practice or sole proprietorship. For the purposes of this book, my references to a "company" refer to a sole proprietorship.

Accordingly, a company is created and owned by a technician, a business is created and owned by a manager, and an enterprise is created and owned by an entrepreneur.

The E-Myth philosophy says that a highly successful real estate investment company can grow into a highly successful real estate investment business, which in turn can become the foundation for an inordinately successful real estate investment enterprise that runs smoothly and efficiently without the real estate investor having to be in the office for ten hours a day, six days a week.

So what is "The E-Myth," exactly? The E-Myth is short for the Entrepreneurial Myth, which says that most businesses fail to fulfill their potential because most people starting their own business are not entrepreneurs at all. They're actually what I call *technicians suffering from an entrepreneurial seizure*. When technicians suffering from an entrepreneurial seizure start a real estate investment company of their own, they almost always end up working themselves into a frenzy; their days are booked solid with appointments. These real estate investors are burning the candle at both ends, fueled by too much coffee and too little sleep, and most of the time, they can't even stop to think.

In short, the E-Myth says that most real estate investors don't own a true business—most own a job. They're doing it, doing it, doing it, hoping like hell to get some time off, but never figuring out how to get their business to run without them. And if your business doesn't run well without you, what happens when you can't be in two places at once? Ultimately, your company will fail.

There are a number of prestigious schools throughout the world dedicated to teaching the science of real estate investment. The problem is they fail to teach the *business* of it. And because no one is being taught how to run a company as a business, some real estate investors find themselves having to close their doors every year. You could be a world-class expert in market valuation, precision marketing, or real estate negotiation, but when it comes to building a successful business all that specified knowledge matters exactly zilch.

The good news is that you don't have to be among the statistics of failure in the real estate investing profession. The E-Myth philosophy I am about to share with you in this book has been successfully applied to thousands of real estate investment companies just like yours with extraordinary results.

The key to transforming your company—and your life—is to grasp the profound difference between going to work on your business (systems thinker) and going to work in your business (tactical thinker). In other words, it's the difference between going to work *on* your business as an entrepreneur and going to work *in* your business as a real estate investor.

The two are not mutually exclusive. In fact, they are essential to each other. The problem with most real estate investment companies is that the systems thinker—the entrepreneur—is completely absent. And so is the vision.

The E-Myth philosophy says that the key to transforming your company into a successful enterprise is knowing how to transform yourself from successful real estate investment technician into successful technician-manager-entrepreneur. In the process, everything you do in your real estate investment company will be transformed. The door is then open to turning it into what it should be—a company, a business, and an enterprise of pure joy.

The E-Myth not only can work for you, it will work for you. In the process, it will give you an entirely new experience of your business and beyond.

To your future and your life. Good reading.

—Michael E. Gerber
Co-Founder/Chairman
Michael E. Gerber Companies, Inc.
Carlsbad, California
www.michaelegerber.com/co-author

ACKNOWLEDGMENTS

Michael E. Gerber

As always, and never to be forgotten, there are those who give of themselves to make my work possible.

To my dearest and most forgiving partner, wife, friend, and co-founder, Luz Delia Gerber, whose love and commitment takes me to places I would often not go unaccompanied.

To Trish Beaulieu, wow, you are splendid.

To Helen Chang, noble warrior, editor, brave soul, and sojourner, who covers all the bases we would have missed had she not been there.

And to Nancy Ratkiewich, whose work has been essential for you who are reading this.

To those many, many dreamers, thinkers, storytellers, and leaders, whose travels with me in The Dreaming Room™ have given me life, breath, and pleasure unanticipated before we met. To those many participants in my life (you know who you are), thank you for taking me seriously, and joining me in this exhilarating quest.

And, of course, to my co-authors, all of you, your genius, wisdom, intelligence, and wit have supplied me with a grand view of the world, which would never have been the same without you.

Love to all.

ACKNOWLEDGMENTS

Than Merrill

I would like to express my deepest gratitude to the many people with whom I've worked with to produce the ideas that are presented in this book. This book is a tribute to your knowledge, insight, and constant support.

To my business partners, Paul Esajian and Konrad Sopielnikow, you deserve as much credit, if not more, for making this book possible. Together, we took an idea to start a business years ago and have made it a much bigger reality than any of us originally expected. Your continued dedication, passion, work ethic, and intensity of purpose are remarkable and something I admire both of you for. I believe our approach of being friends first and business partners second is the key to our success.

To all my team members at FortuneBuilders.com and CT Homes, it is because of you that I wake up every day excited about work, our businesses, and life in general. Together, we have created an amazing, talented family of like-minded individuals who all seek constant daily improvement, and you motivate me to get better every single day.

To all our thousands of clients over the years who are part of our coaching program and have contributed to the success of the Mastery coaching community. Together, we have created a family of highly successful people who are continually sharing ideas and helping each other every single day.

To Helen Chang, my editor, without you this book would have taken a decade. Thank you for your hard work, perfectionism, and constant prodding.

To Cindy Phillips, my wife, partner, and best friend. You have been and will continue to be the single greatest influence in my life. Your intellect, opinion, advice, and caring heart are what I cherish the most. You are my everything.

And finally, to you reading this book. I thank you for your support and enthusiasm and look forward to hearing about your success.

ACKNOWLEDGMENTS

Paul Esajian

I am grateful for the loving support of my family—my wife Andrea and my sons Bruce and Vince.

INTRODUCTION

Michael E. Gerber

A s I write this book, the aftermath of the recession and the slow economic recovery continue to take its toll on American businesses. Like any other industry, real estate investment is not immune. Real estate investors all over the country are watching as home inventory remains tight and there's a lot of competition for a few good deals.

Faced with a struggling economy and tighter funding requirements, many real estate investors I've met are asking themselves, "Why did I ever become a real estate investor in the first place?"

And it isn't just a money problem. After thirty-five years of working with small businesses, many of them real estate investment companies, I'm convinced that the dissatisfaction experienced by countless real estate investors is not just about money. To be frank, the recession doesn't deserve all the blame, either. While the financial crisis our country faced certainly hasn't made things any better, the problem started long before the economy tanked. Let's dig a little deeper. Let's go back to school.

Can you remember that far back? Whichever university or college of real estate investment you attended, you probably had some great teachers who helped you become the fine real estate investor you are. These schools excel at teaching the science of real estate investing; they'll teach you everything you need to know about research and acquisitions, rehab management and bookkeeping. But what they *don't* teach is the consummate skill set needed to be a successful real estate investor, and they certainly don't teach what it takes to build a successful real estate investment enterprise.

Obviously, something is seriously wrong. The education that real estate investment professionals receive in school doesn't go far enough, deep enough, broad enough. Real estate college programs don't teach you how to relate to the *enterprise* of real estate investment or to the *business* of real estate investment; they only teach you how to relate to the *practice* of real estate investing. In other words, they merely teach you how to be an *effective* rather than a *successful* real estate investor. Last time I checked, they weren't offering degrees in success. That's why most real estate investors are effective, but few are successful.

Although a successful real estate investor must be effective, an effective real estate investor does not have to be—and in most cases isn't—successful.

An effective real estate investor is capable of executing his or her duties with as much certainty and professionalism as possible.

A successful real estate investor, on the other hand, works balanced hours, has little stress, leads rich and rewarding relationships with friends and family, and has an economic life that is diverse, fulfilling, and shows a continuous return on investment.

A successful real estate investor finds time and ways to give back to the community but at little cost to his or her sense of ease.

A successful real estate investor is a leader, not simply someone who teaches novices real estate investing, but a sage; a rich person (in the broadest sense of the word); a strong father, mother, wife, or husband; a friend, teacher, mentor, and spiritually grounded human being; and a person who can see clearly into all aspects of what it means to lead a fulfilling life.

So let's go back to the original question. Why did you become a real estate investor? Were you striving to just be an effective one, or did you dream about real and resounding success?

I don't know how you've answered that question in the past, but I am confident that once you understand the strategic thinking laid out in this book, you will answer it differently in the future.

If the ideas here are going to be of value to you, it's critical that you begin to look at yourself in a different, more productive way. I am suggesting that you go beyond the mere technical aspects of your daily job as a real estate investor and begin instead to think strategically about your real estate investment company as both a business and an enterprise.

I often say that most *companies* don't work—the people who own them do. In other words, most real estate investment companies are jobs for the real estate investors who own them. Does this sound familiar? The real estate investor, overcome by an entrepreneurial seizure, has started his or her own company, become his or her own boss, and now works for a lunatic!

The result: the real estate investor is running out of time, patience, and ultimately money. Not to mention paying the worst price anyone can pay for the inability to understand what a true company is, what a true business is, and what a true enterprise is—the price of his or her life.

In this book I'm going to make the case for why you should think differently about what you do and why you do it. It isn't just the future of your real estate investment company that hangs in the balance. It's the future of your life.

The E-Myth Real Estate Investor is an exciting departure from my other sole-authored books. In this book, an expert—a successful real estate investor who has successfully applied the E-Myth to the development of his real estate investment company—is sharing his secrets about how he achieved extraordinary results using the E-Myth paradigm. In addition to the time-tested E-Myth strategies and systems I'll be sharing with you, you'll benefit from the wisdom, guidance, and practical tips provided by a legion of real estate investors who've been in your shoes.

The problems that afflict real estate investment companies today don't only exist in the field of real estate investing; the same problems are confronting every organization of every size, in every industry in every country in the world. *The E-Myth Real Estate Investor* is next in a new series of E-Myth Expert books that will serve as a launching pad for Michael E. Gerber Partners™ to bring a legacy of expertise to small, struggling businesses in *all* industries. This series will offer an exciting opportunity to understand and apply the significance of E-Myth methodology in both theory and practice to businesses in need of development and growth.

The E-Myth says that only by conducting your *business* in a truly innovative and independent way will you ever realize the unmatched joy that comes from creating a truly independent business, a business that works *without* you rather than *because* of you.

The E-Myth says that it is only by learning the difference between the work of a *business* and the business of *work* that real estate investors will be freed from the predictable and often overwhelming tyranny of the unprofitable, unproductive routine that consumes them on a daily basis.

The E-Myth says that what will make the ultimate difference between the success or failure of your real estate investment company is first and foremost how you *think* about your business, as opposed to how hard you work in it.

So, let's think it through together. Let's think about those things—work, clients, money, time—that dominate the world of real estate investors everywhere.

Let's talk about planning. About growth. About management. About getting a life!

Let's think about improving your and your family's life through the development of an extraordinary company. About getting the life you've always dreamed of but never thought you could actually have.

Envision the future you want, and the future is yours.

CHAPTER

1

The Story of Steve and Peggy

Michael E. Gerber

You leave home to seek your fortune and, when you get it, you go home and share it with your family.

—Anita Baker

E very business is a family business. To ignore this truth is to court disaster.

This is true whether or not family members actually work in the business. Whatever their relationship with the business, every member of a real estate investor's family will be greatly affected by the decisions a real estate investor makes about the business. There's just no way around it.

Unfortunately, like most businessmen, real estate investors tend to compartmentalize their lives. They view their business as a profession—what they do—and therefore it's none of their family's business.

"This has nothing to do with you," says the real estate investor to his wife, with blind conviction. "I leave work at the office and family at home."

1

2 The E-Myth Real Estate Investor

And with equal conviction, I say, "Not true!"

In actuality, your family and investment company are inextricably linked to one another. What's happening in your company is also happening at home. Consider the following and ask yourself if each is true:

- If you're angry at work, you're also angry at home.
- If you're out of control at your real estate investment company, you're equally out of control at home.
- If you're having trouble with money at your company, you're also having trouble with money at home.
- If you have communication problems at your company, you're also having communication problems at home.
- If you don't trust in your company, you don't trust at home.
- If you're secretive at your company, you're equally secretive at home.

And you're paying a huge price for it!

The truth is that your company and your family are one—and you're the link. Or you should be. Because if you try to keep your company and your family apart, if your company and your family are strangers, you will effectively create two separate worlds that can never wholeheartedly serve each other. Two worlds that split each other apart.

Let me tell you the story of Steve and Peggy Walsh.

The Walshes met in college. They were partners in a study club for a finance class—Steve a business administration student and Peggy in architecture. When their discussions started to wander beyond market analysis and investment theory and into their personal lives, they discovered they had a lot in common. By the end of the course, they weren't just talking in class; they were talking on the phone every night . . . and *not* about finance.

Steve thought Peggy was absolutely brilliant, and Peggy considered Steve the most passionate man she knew. It wasn't long before they were engaged and planning their future together. A week after graduation, they were married in a lovely garden ceremony in Peggy's childhood home.

While Steve studied business administration at a prestigious college, Peggy entered an architecture masters program nearby. Over the next few years, the couple worked hard to keep their finances afloat. They worked long hours and studied constantly; they were often exhausted and struggled to make ends meet. But through it all, they were committed to what they were doing and to each other.

After graduating, Steve became a real estate agent in a busy real estate investment company while Peggy began working in a large architecture firm nearby. Soon afterward, the couple had their first son, and Peggy decided to take some time off to be with him. Those were good years. Steve and Peggy loved each other very much, were active members in their church, participated in community organizations, and spent quality time together. The Walshes considered themselves one of the most fortunate families they knew.

But work became troublesome. Steve grew increasingly frustrated with the way the company was run. "I want to go into business for myself," he announced one night at the dinner table. "I want to start my own company."

Steve and Peggy spent many nights talking about the move. Was it something they could afford? Did Steve really have the skills necessary to make a real estate investment company a success? Were there enough clients and deals to go around? What impact would such a move have on Peggy's career at the architect firm, their lifestyle, their son, their relationship? They asked all the questions they thought they needed to answer before Steve went into business for himself . . . but they never really drew up a concrete plan.

Finally, tired of talking and confident that he could handle whatever he might face, Steve committed to starting his own real estate investment company. Because she loved and supported him, Peggy agreed, offering her own commitment to help in any way she could. So Steve quit his job, took out a second mortgage on their home, and leased a small office nearby.

In the beginning, things went well. A building boom had hit the town, and new families were pouring into the area. Steve had no trouble getting new clients. His company expanded, quickly outgrowing his office.

Within a year, Steve had employed an office manager, Clarissa, to run the front desk and handle the administrative side of the business. He also hired a bookkeeper, Tim, to handle the finances. Steve was ecstatic with the progress his young company had made. He celebrated by taking his wife and son on vacation to Italy.

Of course, managing a business was more complicated and time-consuming than working for someone else. Steve not only supervised all the jobs Clarissa and Tim did, but also was continually looking for work to keep everyone busy. When he wasn't scanning journals of real estate investment to stay abreast of what was going on in the field or attending industry events to stay current, he was going to the bank, wading through client paperwork, or speaking with mortgage companies (which usually degenerated into arguing with mortgage companies). He also found himself spending more and more time on the telephone dealing with client complaints and nurturing relationships.

As the months went by and more and more clients came through the door, Steve had to spend even more time just trying to keep his head above water.

By the end of its second year, the company, now employing two full-time and two part-time people, had moved to a larger office downtown. The demands on Steve's time had grown with the company.

He began leaving home earlier in the morning and returning later at night. He drank more. He rarely saw his son anymore. For the most part, Steve was resigned to the problem. He saw the hard work as essential to building the "sweat equity" he had long heard about.

Money was also becoming a problem for Steve. Although the company was growing like crazy, money always seemed scarce when it was really needed.

When Steve had worked for somebody else, he had been paid twice a month. In his own company, he often had to wait—sometimes for months. Even if a property were in escrow, buyers and sellers sometimes could not come to terms, the buyer didn't qualify for mortgages, and deals fell through. Of course, no matter how slowly Steve got paid, he still had to pay *his* people. This became a relentless problem. Steve often felt like a juggler dancing on a tightrope. A fire burned in his stomach day and night.

To make matters worse, Steve began to feel that Peggy was insensitive to his troubles. Not that he often talked to his wife about the company. "Business is business" was Steve's mantra. "It's my responsibility to handle things at the office and Peggy's responsibility to take care of her own job and the family."

Peggy was working late hours at the architecture firm, and they'd brought in a nanny to help with their son. Steve couldn't help but notice that his wife seemed resentful, and her apparent lack of understanding baffled him. Didn't she see that he had a company to take care of? That he was doing it all for his family? Apparently not.

As time went on, Steve became even more consumed and frustrated by his company. When he went off on his own, he remembered saying, "I don't like people telling me what to do." But people were still telling him what to do.

Not surprisingly, Peggy grew more frustrated by her husband's lack of communication. She cut back on her own hours at the architecture firm to focus on their family, but her husband still never seemed to be around. Their relationship grew tense and strained. The rare moments they *were* together were more often than not peppered by long silences—a far cry from the heartfelt conversations that had characterized their relationship's early days, when they'd talk into the wee hours of the morning.

Meanwhile, Tim, the bookkeeper, was also becoming a problem for Steve. Tim never seemed to have the financial information Steve needed to make decisions about payroll, billing, and general operating expenses, let alone how much money was available for Steve and Peggy's living expenses.

When questioned, Tim would shift his gaze to his feet and say, "Listen, Steve, I've got a lot more to do around here than you can imagine. It'll take a little more time. Just don't press me, okay?"

Overwhelmed by his own work, Steve usually backed off. The last thing Steve wanted was to upset Tim and have to do the books himself. He could also empathize with what Tim was going through, given the company's growth over the past year.

Late at night in his office, Steve would sometimes recall his first years out of school. He missed the simple life he and his family had shared. Then, as quickly as the thoughts came, they would vanish. He had work to do and no time for daydreaming. "Having my own company is a great thing," he would remind himself. "I simply have to apply myself, as I did in school, and get on with the job. I have to work as hard as I always have when something needed to get done."

Steve began to live most of his life inside his head. He began to distrust his people. They never seemed to work hard enough or to care about his company as much as he did. If he wanted to go get something done, he usually had to do it himself.

Then one day, the office manager, Clarissa, quit in a huff, frustrated by the amount of work that her boss was demanding of her. Steve was left with a desk full of papers and a telephone that wouldn't stop ringing.

Clueless about the work Clarissa had done, Steve was overwhelmed by having to pick up the pieces of a job he didn't understand. His world turned upside down. He felt like a stranger in his own company.

Why had he been such a fool? Why hadn't he taken the time to learn what Clarissa did in the office? Why had he waited until now?

Ever the trouper, Steve plowed into Clarissa's job with everything he could muster. What he found shocked him. Clarissa's work space was a disaster area! Her desk drawers were a jumble of papers, coins, pens, pencils, rubber bands, envelopes, business cards, fee slips, eye drops, and candy.

"What was she thinking?" Steve raged.

When he got home that night, even later than usual, he got into a shouting match with Peggy. He settled it by storming out of the house to get a drink. Didn't anybody understand him? Didn't anybody care what he was going through?

He returned home only when he was sure Peggy was asleep. He slept on the couch and left early in the morning, before anyone was awake. He was in no mood for questions or arguments. When Steve got to his office the next morning, he immediately headed for the break room, where he could put his head down to soothe his throbbing headache.

What lessons can we draw from Steve and Peggy's story? I've said it once and I'll say it again: *Every business is a family business*. Your business profoundly touches all members of your family, even if they never set foot inside your office. Every business either gives to the family or takes from the family, just as individual family members do.

If the business takes more than it gives, the family is always the first to pay the price.

In order for Steve to free himself from the prison he created, he would first have to admit his vulnerability. He would have to confess to himself and his family that he really didn't know enough about his own company and how to grow it.

Steve tried to do it all himself. Had he succeeded, had the company supported his family in the style he imagined, he would have burst with pride. Instead, Steve unwittingly isolated himself, thereby achieving the exact opposite of what he sought.

He destroyed his life—and his family's life along with it.

Repeat after me: *Every business is a family business*.

Are you like Steve? I believe that all real estate investors share a common soul with him. You must learn that a business is only a business. It is not your life. But it is also true that your business can have a profoundly negative impact on your life unless you learn how to do it differently than most real estate investors do it—and definitely differently than Steve did it.

Steve's real estate investment company could have served his and his family's life. But for that to happen, he would have had to learn how to master his company in a way that was completely foreign to him.

Instead, Steve's company consumed him. Because he lacked a true understanding of the essential strategic thinking that would

 the story I just told you.
Let's talk about Than and Paul's journey . . . and yours. ❧

www.michaelegerber.com/co-author

CHAPTER 2

The Real Estate Investor's Journey

Than Merrill
Paul Esajian

Life is a journey, not a destination —we determine our destiny by the direction we take.

—Anonymous

Again, our business systems are the collective experience of all our partners, but for simplicity's sake this story is told from Than's voice alone. When we were in our early twenties, we three partners decided we didn't want to have a job or work for somebody else. We didn't want to have someone else determining the income we could earn or what type of lifestyle we could chose to live. So we decided to go into real estate, where we saw we could have this type of lifestyle independence.

But we knew that we had to first learn the business. We decided to educate ourselves about the industry as a whole and the real estate investing business in particular. So we devoured as many real estate books as we could, attended every seminar possible, and found other, more-experienced investors whom we could model ourselves after. Through those shared experiences and our continuing desire for further education, we launched our business.

Misguided Thinking

The first problem was we believed —like most small-business owners and entrepreneurs do—that all we needed was an education on the mechanics of the real estate deal. We thought: "OK, if we learn how to find good deals and learn how to analyze those deals, if we learn how to raise money for those deals and learn how to manage the rehab (renovation) process and the sales process, then we are going to be successful."

Unfortunately, we were flat out wrong. The one thing we didn't understand is that it is a business and needs to be treated and run like a business.

Most real estate education seminars, books, and curricula created by successful real estate investors focus purely on the mechanics of how to do the business yourself. And that's the biggest distinguishing factor marking our journey from when we started to where we are now. When we started, we were the business. If you took us out of the equation, the business produced no income.

Most real estate investing—in fact, we would guess 97 percent—is composed of what is considered mom-and-pop investors: people who are working in their business every single day. And most real estate investors are willing to put up with this mind-numbing stress. Most of them don't manage risk well and haven't created a successful business model. They have created for themselves essentially nothing more than a highly lucrative job, instead of financial freedom and the lifestyle that comes with it.

Key Discoveries

It took us about a year to realize that we needed to make serious and significant changes in how we ran our business if we wanted to create financial freedom for ourselves. We realized we didn't have any competitive advantages and that we were our business. From that moment, we made some monumental shifts in our approach to the business in order to grow and scale and eventually "free us" from the business itself. Let us share some of these key lessons with you!

Key Lesson 1: Accumulate Specific Knowledge

A century ago, if you wanted to master something you would go apprentice with someone who had years of experience. Now, in most professions, you can go down established education and career tracks. You go to school for a certain number of years, pursue and achieve a degree or a designation, and then more often than not you end up working for someone else for some years to learn the profession.

That's not the case for the majority of real estate investors. There are some real estate MBA programs, but most major universities don't have a degree program. Consequently, most real estate investors have to learn through experience. Many of them are real estate agents who start investing from their own portfolio.

Without a traditional career track, so much of your success is based on your desire to self-educate. Most successful investors acquire knowledge through books, seminars, and trainings. That gives you the confidence and a foundation on how real estate transactions are to be completed.

What's important to understand is that this educational process never stops. It's very much like working out. You can't expect to spend a week in the gym and be fit for life. Obviously, it would be absurd to think that way. Still, a lot of people think that a week-long class is all they need to be successful in real estate. Those are the people who usually never do anything significant or lose significant money as investors.

All of us realized that knowledge accumulation is an ongoing process. The market is mercurial, legislation changes constantly, technology evolves rapidly, and new opportunities are always coming up. We made a commitment to spend a few hours each week educating ourselves about our profession—and we continue to do it to this day. Looking back it is one of the best commitments we made early on in our careers.

Key Lesson 2: Gain Intimate Market Knowledge

It doesn't matter where you invest; there are always opportunities in every market, in every cycle, no matter what happens in the local or national economy. The key is to really understand the unique aspects of your market and acquire local market knowledge. This process starts by understanding price points on the types of properties you will be acquiring. Your intimate market knowledge can also be a competitive advantage for your business because you will be able to spot opportunities others investors don't. You will also be able to move faster than your competitors because you will be able to recognize good deals faster.

We lost quite a few good deals in our first year of business to other investors who had superior market knowledge. Often times a property would hit the market or the seller would contact us looking for an offer and we were too slow in our analysis and ended up losing the deal. So we decided we needed to get more dialed in to what was happening in our market. Here's how you can do the same.

The first step is to understand price points of property types you are focusing on by area. For example, if you are focused on median-priced homes it would be a good idea to get a huge map of the area, put it on your wall, and then start sectioning off areas based on common price points. For example, you may find one neighborhood where houses generally sell for $200,000 to $250,000. But in another development up the hill, houses sell for $300,000 to $400,000. This map will give you a good feel for not only your area, but for the sale prices within smaller sections of town.

The next thing you should do is pick up a local zoning map for the areas you are buying in. There are many opportunities you will discover based on what area the property is located in and what the zoning laws are for that type of property. Let's say you are considering buying a duplex, and you find out the area is zoned for residential and commercial properties. You could potentially turn that duplex into an office space and rent it out for a higher amount. We would advise you to attend a few planning and zoning meetings in your area because you will learn a lot about new developments being planned and the process in general.

The final thing we would recommend is that you take a real estate appraisal class in your area. It may not be the most exciting class you have ever taken, but the knowledge of how appraisers value property in your area is invaluable. You can use this information to evaluate properties that you are making offers on.

Key Lesson 3: Focus on a Market Niche

One of the fundamental shifts we made in our business was when we decided to specialize in certain niches of the market. During our first year in the business, we evaluated and made offers on all types of properties without focusing on anything. Eventually, we made a conscious decision to specialize in certain types instead of being a real estate jack of all trades. It was one of the best decisions we made because it allowed us to focus, grow, and scale rather than jump around from one type of property to another.

We decided to specialize in rehabbing single-family and multifamily properties that needed extensive work and were in median-income areas. We found that there was a lot less competition among our competitors for the bigger rehab projects. Most of the investors in our area wanted to buy, fix, and sell properties that required less than

$30,000 in work so we focused on the bigger projects. We were also able to pick these larger projects up at much deeper discounts so our average profit per deal was much higher than that of our competitors.

Our choice to specialize in larger rehab projects meant each project was going to take longer and require more capital. It also was going to require a deeper understanding of the construction process. However, we knew that after we mastered this niche of the market we were going to have a competitive advantage over other investors because we would feel comfortable taking on increasingly bigger and more profitable development projects. We also discovered that our superior knowledge of construction would enable us to get rehab projects completed faster and cheaper than our competitors could. We quickly became the largest residential redevelopment company in the area because of this decision.

No matter the area of your business, we suggest you make the conscious decision to specialize in only one or two sectors of real estate at a time. Let your knowledge of real estate, knowledge of the market, and your desired lifestyle lead you to this decision. If you try to invest in many different sectors at once you can easily lose your focus and the odds may work against you. It is also much easier to automate a business and remove yourself from your business if you specialize because you can train others to replace you.

Key Lesson 4: Become a Private-Money Raising Machine

It goes without saying that having access to a lot of capital for your real estate deals, your business working capital, and your education are very important. What's also important is that you realize it doesn't have to be your money that you use for investments.

In fact, if you truly understand the business, you can borrow millions of dollars for your deals regardless of your current financials or credit score. That is because you will target private lenders, as we call them in the real estate investment world, and utilize their funds to run your business and fund your deals.

Private lenders are individuals with money. They could be friends and family or people in your community who have money and are looking for a good rate of return on their money. Essentially, private lenders take the place of a bank and fund the purchase and construction of the properties you buy. There is no set standard when it comes to private lending; however most of the time the loans will be for very short periods of between six and twelve months.

Typically, private money lenders will want between 6 percent and 12 percent interest on their money. In exchange for lending you the money for the deal, you will give them a promissory note and a mortgage or deed of trust on the property. Likewise, they will be named in the insurance policy in case something happens to the property while you own it. Finally, some private lenders will want you to "personally guarantee" the loan—meaning the loan is secured by your own house or other assets— but everything is negotiable.

Early on, we realized that having relationships with private lenders would give us an advantage over competitors who had not taken the time to develop such relationships. These relationships not only gave us the confidence to make more offers, and do more deals, but they also insulated us from a lot of risk, because the access to additional funds gave our business more liquidity.

By utilizing private lenders we also could borrow at lower interest rates with even more flexible terms than other investors in the area. This gave us a significant advantage because we didn't have to spend a lot of time jumping through hoops trying to qualify for loans with banks or other non-traditional lenders—and risk losing deals in the process. Essentially, private lenders gave us more flexibility when making offers.

Over the years, as we have built cash reserves, we have found private lending to be a great way to also keep earning high rates of return from our business profits, instead of just keeping them in the bank for dismal returns. So believe us when we tell you that private money is the best source of financing for deals; investors like us prefer to lend money to other investors in return for rates that beat the banks.

Key Lesson 5: Develop Systems

Years ago, after we completed our first few deals we decided we wanted to start growing our business. Many of you reading this book will go through this same thought process. We knew that in order to become more profitable we had to become more efficient with the time we were spending working in the business. We also knew, from reading *The E-Myth*, that we had to create systems in order to do this. Our goal was simple: we wanted to "shrink" the average time it took us to complete a deal.

To accomplish this goal we divided the business into departments and then deconstructed a few of our past transactions step-by-step. We looked for more efficient ways to manage each step of the transaction from marketing to sale. If a checklist was needed we created it, if a mind map (visual outline) was needed to organize information we developed it, and if technology would save time we implemented it. Along the way we created very detailed standard operating procedures that we have continued to use and tweak to this day. The next chapters give examples of such systems.

We also created positions to handle these different aspects of the business so that we could begin to remove ourselves from much of the day-to-day work.

Key Lesson 6: Scale Your Business

As our real estate business became more streamlined through the systems and technology we created and implemented, our appetite for growth continued. We knew that the only way to grow further was to hire talented team members to replace ourselves. We had the confidence to do this because we had developed very detailed systems and standard operating procedures that other people could follow, even without any experience. Now it was just a matter of interviewing, hiring, and training the most-talented people we could find. It is such an important topic that we have devoted a whole chapter in this book to the details of this process.

The bottom line is that if you truly want to grow your real estate business it will require you to learn more than just how to buy and sell real estate deals. First, you have to use your personal time working "in" the business as strategically as possible. Second, you must spend a lot of time educating yourself on running a business and financial management. Finally, you will have to learn how to hire and manage talented people effectively, which we will discuss in Chapter 12.

Key Lesson 7: Create Additional Streams of Income

Early on, we realized that there are a lot of income streams that can be developed outside of just acquiring and selling properties. A lot of people you come into contact with in the daily course of your business will never sell to you or buy a property from you. However, you can absolutely influence them and provide other real estate-related products and services through a network of affiliate relationships that you develop. Affiliate relationships are when at least two people or organizations promote the same product or service.

For example, let's say you are a personal trainer with a website promoting your fitness services. Your colleague has a book about diet and exercise that she wants to sell via your website. For every book that's sold through your website, she's willing to give you 30 percent of the cover price.

Like in the above example, the commissions or referral fees tend to range from 10 percent to 50 percent. As you can imagine, affiliate relationships can generate a lot of income for you and your business. In fact, in our second year of investing, we covered our marketing and overhead costs simply by referring people we met and formed relationships with those selling ancillary real estate-related services and products.

We earned referral commissions from tons of sellers who weren't motivated enough to sell their property at a discount, but were still very realistic about the price. We now refer those leads to our own real estate brokerage and the agents who work under us. Likewise, we have referred and continue to refer buyers to hard money lenders, credit repair companies, home warranty companies, etc., and have made a lot of money from this over the years.

Key Lesson 8: Create Passive Income Streams

Over the years we made a strategic choice to also build our rental property portfolio to take advantage of the many long-term benefits of owning real estate. To this day we continue to build this portfolio every month. We have financed the majority of these acquisitions using the profits from the properties we flip.

When we started out, our goal was to use this monthly passive cash flow to take care of our living expenses and office overhead. We have also benefited from the significant tax advantages, mortgage principal reduction, and long-term appreciation.

Change this target range to reflect our changes cash-on-cash return, and are in strong markets, where we have a great property management team.

We can't stress enough the importance of taking the same approach with your real estate business. As your monthly cash flow grows, your business will become more sustainable and predictable because you can begin to rely on that cash flow to make sound business decisions. Your cash flow also makes you more attractive to banks and lenders when you are looking for bank lines of credit and financing for your other property acquisitions. Banks prefer predictability as opposed to the sometime unpredictable world of flipping properties. More importantly, you will have more peace of mind when you are vacationing with your family in Bermuda and the money is still rolling in. Cheers to that!

Key Lesson 9: Remove Yourself from Your Business

The last key lesson we would like to share is how we strategically began removing ourselves from different parts of our business. Ultimately, the goal of this book is to show you how to strategically build your real estate business so you can eventually remove yourself from your business.

Our approach was systematic, but it is not an overnight process. First, we believe you have to master your craft in each department of your business yourself—such as sales, marketing, operations, rehab, financing and so on—to gain a deep enough understanding of "how" the business works. At the same time, you design systems to make the time you spend "in" the business as efficient as possible. Then you create standard operating and training procedures, so you can train someone to replace you in the different divisions of the business.

We made a conscious goal to meet every quarter to review not only our personal performances, but also the systems we were developing to begin this removal process. Every quarter, beginning in our second year, we made it a goal to either hire someone to replace ourselves or expand one of our employee's roles and responsibilities so they could take over a new area of the business. This was a difficult, but very rewarding, process because we learned how to achieve our goals while at the same time help other people to achieve theirs.

Wrapping It Up

Looking back, all these lessons played a vital role in our personal journeys to financial freedom. Each lesson was a fundamental shift in the way we ran our business and ultimately played a role in how we were able to free ourselves from the drudgery of work that plagues most real estate investors. The great thing is that this doesn't have to happen to you if you model our business and leverage the systems we have already created. We tell our coaching students all the time that there is no need to reinvent the wheel when it comes to starting their real estate businesses.

So please heed our advice, commit to reading each chapter in this book, and ultimately implement what we teach so you can design the real estate business of your dreams and get your life back.

Let's move on to the next chapter and let's find out what Michael has to teach us about money. ✤

For more information about how we can help you as a real estate investor go to: www.MasteryForInvestors.com.

On the Subject of Money

Michael E. Gerber

There are three faithful friends: an old wife, an old dog, and ready money.
—Benjamin Franklin

Had Steve and Peggy first considered the subject of *money* as we will here, their lives could have been radically different.

Money is on the tip of every real estate investor's tongue, on the edge (or at the very center) of every real estate investor's thoughts, intruding on every part of a real estate investor's life.

With money consuming so much energy, why do so few real estate investors handle it well? Why was Steve, like so many real estate investors, willing to entrust his financial affairs to a relative stranger? Why is money scarce for most real estate investors? Why is there less money than expected? And yet the demand for money is *always* greater than anticipated.

What is it about money that is so elusive, so complicated, so difficult to control? Why is it that every real estate investor I've ever met hates to deal with the subject of money? Why are they almost always too late in facing money problems? And why are they constantly obsessed with the desire for more of it?

Money—you can't live with it and you can't live without it. But you'd better understand it and get your people to understand it. Because until you do, money problems will eat your company for lunch.

You don't need an accountant or financial planner to do this. You simply need to prod your people to relate to money very personally. From the real estate agent technician to the rehab project manager, they all should understand the financial impact of what they do every day in relationship to the profit and loss of the company.

And so you must teach your people to think like owners, not like technicians or office managers or receptionists. You must teach them to operate like personal profit centers, with a sense of how their work fits in with the company as a whole.

You must involve everyone in the company with the topic of money—how it works, where it goes, how much is left, and how much everybody gets at the end of the day. You also must teach them about the four kinds of money created by the company.

The Four Kinds of Money

In the context of owning, operating, developing, and exiting from a real estate investment company, money can be split into four distinct but highly integrated categories:

- Income
- Profit
- Flow
- Equity

Failure to distinguish how the four kinds of money play out in your company is a surefire recipe for disaster.

Important Note: Do not talk to your accountants or bookkeepers about what follows; it will only confuse them and you. The information comes from the real-life experiences of thousands of small-business owners, real estate investors included, most of who were hopelessly confused about money when I met them. Once they understood and accepted the following principles, they developed a clarity about money that could only be called enlightened.

The First Kind of Money: Income

Income is the money real estate investors are paid by their company for doing their job *in* the company. It's what they get paid for going to work every day.

Clearly, if real estate investors didn't do their job, others would have to, and *they* would be paid the money the company currently pays the real estate investors. Income, then, has nothing to do with *ownership*. Income is solely the province of *employee-ship*.

That's why to the real estate investor-as-*employee*, income is the most important form money can take. To the real estate investor-as-*owner*, however, it is the least important form money can take.

Most important; least important. Do you see the conflict? The conflict between the real estate investor-as-employee and the real estate investor-as-owner?

We'll deal with this conflict later. For now, just know that it is potentially the most paralyzing conflict in a real estate investor's life.

Failing to resolve this conflict will cripple you. Resolving it will set you free.

The Second Kind of Money: Profit

Profit is what's left over after a real estate investment company has done its job effectively and efficiently. If there is no profit, the company is doing something wrong.

However, just because the company shows a profit does not mean it is necessarily doing all the right things in the right way. Instead, it just means that something was done right during or preceding the period in which the profit was earned.

The important issue here is whether the profit was intentional or accidental. If it happened by accident (which most profit does), don't take credit for it. You'll live to regret your impertinence.

If it happened intentionally, take all the credit you want. You've earned it. Because profit created intentionally, rather than by accident, is replicable—again and again. And your company's ability to repeat its performance is the most critical ability it can have.

As you'll soon see, the value of money is a function of your company's ability to produce it in predictable amounts at an above-average return on investment.

Profit can be understood only in the context of your company's purpose, as opposed to your purpose as a real estate investor. Profit, then, fuels the forward motion of the company that produces it. This is accomplished in four ways:

- Profit is *investment capital* that feeds and supports growth.
- Profit is *bonus capital* that rewards people for exceptional work.
- Profit is *operating capital* that shores up money shortfalls.
- Profit is *return-on-investment capital* that rewards you, the real estate investor-owner, for taking risks.

Without profit, a real estate investment company cannot subsist, much less grow. Profit is the fuel of progress.

If a company misuses or abuses profit, however, the penalty is much like having no profit at all. Imagine the plight of a real estate investor who has way too much return-on-investment capital and not enough investment capital, bonus capital, and operating capital. Can you see the imbalance this creates?

The Third Kind of Money: Flow

Flow is what money *does* in a real estate investment company, as opposed to what money *is*. Whether the company is large or small, money tends to move erratically through it, much like a pinball. One minute it's there; the next minute it's not.

Flow can be even more critical to a company's survival than profit, because a company can produce a profit and still be short of money. Has this ever happened to you? It's called profit on paper rather than in fact.

No matter how large your company, if the money isn't there when it's needed, you're threatened—regardless of how much profit you've made. You can borrow it, of course. But money acquired in dire circumstances is almost always the most expensive kind of money you can get.

Knowing where the money is and where it will be when you need it is a critically important task of both the real estate investor-as-employee and the real estate investor-as-owner.

Rules of Flow

You will learn no more important lesson than the huge impact flow can have on the health and survival of your real estate investment company, let alone your business or enterprise. The following two rules will help you understand why this subject is so critical.

1. **The First Rule of Flow states that your income statement is static, while the flow is dynamic.** Your income statement is a snapshot, while the flow is a moving picture. So, while your income statement is an excellent tool for analyzing your company *after* the fact, it's a poor tool for managing it in the heat of the moment.

Your income statement tells you (1) how much money you're spending and where, and (2) how much money you're receiving and from where.

Flow gives you the same information as the income statement, plus it tells you *when* you're spending and receiving money. In other words, flow is an income statement moving through time. And that is the key to understanding flow. It is about management in real time. How much is coming in? How much is going out? You'd like to know this daily, or even by the hour if possible. Never by the week or month.

You must be able to forecast flow. You must have a flow plan that helps you gain a clear vision of the money that's out there next month and the month after that. You must also pinpoint what your needs will be in the future.

Ultimately, however, when it comes to flow, the action is always in the moment. It's about *now*. The minute you start to meander away from the present, you'll miss the boat.

Unfortunately, few real estate investors pay any attention to flow until it dries up completely and slow pay becomes no pay. They are oblivious to this kind of detail until, say, a contract to buy falls through. That gets a real estate investor's attention because the expenses keep on coming.

When it comes to flow, most real estate investors are flying by the proverbial seat of their pants. No matter how many people you hire to take care of your money, until you change the way you think about it, you will always be out of luck. No one can do this for you.

Managing flow takes attention to detail. But when flow is managed, your life takes on an incredible sheen. You're swimming with the current, not against it. You're in charge!

2. **The Second Rule of Flow states that money seldom moves as you expect it to.** But you do have the power to change that, provided you understand the two primary sources of money as it comes in and goes out of your real estate investment company.

The truth is, the more control you have over the *source* of money, the more control you have over its flow. The sources of money are both inside and outside your company.

Money comes from *outside* your company in the form of receivables, commissions, reimbursements, investments, and loans.

Money comes from *inside* your company in the form of payables, taxes, capital investments, and payroll. These are the costs associated with attracting clients, delivering your services, operations, and so forth.

Few real estate investors see the money going *out* of their company as a source of money, but it is.

When considering how to spend money in your company, you can save—and therefore make—money in three ways:

- Do it more effectively.
- Do it more efficiently.
- Stop doing it altogether.

By identifying the money sources inside and outside your company, and then applying these methods, you will be immeasurably better at controlling the flow in your company.

But what are these sources? They include how you

- manage your services;
- buy supplies and equipment;
- compensate your people;
- plan people's use of time;
- determine the direct cost of your services;
- increase the number of clients seen;
- manage your work;
- collect reimbursements and receivables; and
- countless more.

In fact, every task performed in your company (and ones you haven't yet learned how to perform) can be done more efficiently and effectively, dramatically reducing the cost of doing business. In the process, you will create more income, produce more profit, and balance the flow.

The Fourth Kind of Money: Equity

Sadly, few real estate investors fully appreciate the value of equity in their real estate investment company. Yet equity is the second most valuable asset any real estate investor will ever possess. (The first most valuable asset is, of course, your life. More on that later.)

Equity is the financial value placed on your real estate investment company by a prospective buyer.

Thus, your *company* is your most important product, not your services. Because your company has the power to set you free. That's right. Once you sell your company—providing you get what you want for it—you're free!

Of course, to enhance your equity, to increase your company's value, you have to build it right. You have to build a company that works. A company that can become a true business and a business that can become a true enterprise. A company/business/enterprise that can produce income, profit, flow, and equity better than any other real estate investor's company can.

To accomplish that, your company must be designed so that it can do what it does systematically and predictably, every single time.

The Story of McDonald's

Let me tell you the most unlikely story anyone has ever told you about the successful building of a real estate investment company, business, and enterprise. Let me tell you the story of Ray Kroc.

You might be thinking, "What on earth does a hamburger stand have to do with my company? I'm not in the hamburger business; I'm a real estate investor."

Yes, you are. But by practicing real estate investing as you have been taught, you've abandoned any chance to expand your reach, help more clients, or improve your services the way they must be improved if the business of real estate investing—and your life—is going to be transformed.

In Ray Kroc's story lies the answer.

Kroc called his first McDonald's restaurant "a little money machine." That's why thousands of franchises bought it. And the reason it worked? Kroc demanded consistency, so that a hamburger in Philadelphia would be an advertisement for one in Peoria. In fact, no matter where you bought a McDonald's hamburger in the 1950s, the meat patty was guaranteed to weigh exactly 1.6 ounces, with a diameter of 3⅝ inches. It was in the McDonald's handbook.

Did Kroc succeed? You know he did! And so can you, once you understand his methods. Consider just one part of his story.

In 1954, Kroc made his living selling the five-spindle Multimixer milkshake machine. He heard about a hamburger stand in San Bernardino, California, that had eight of his machines in operation, meaning it could make forty shakes simultaneously. This he had to see.

Kroc flew from Chicago to Los Angeles, then drove 60 miles to San Bernardino. As he sat in his car outside Mac and Dick McDonald's restaurant, he watched as lunch customers lined up for bags of hamburgers.

In a revealing moment, Kroc approached a strawberry blonde in a yellow convertible. As he later described it, "It was not her sex appeal but the obvious relish with which she devoured the hamburger that made my pulse begin to hammer with excitement."

Passion.

In fact, it was the French fry that truly captured his heart. Before the 1950s, it was almost impossible to buy fries of consistent quality. Kroc changed all that. "The French fry," he once wrote, "would become almost sacrosanct for me, its preparation a ritual to be followed religiously."

Passion and preparation.

The potatoes had to be just so—top-quality Idaho russets, 8 ounces apiece, deep-fried to a golden brown, and salted with a shaker that, as Kroc put it, kept going "like a Salvation Army girl's tambourine."

As Kroc soon learned, potatoes too high in water content—even top-quality Idaho russets varied greatly in water content—will come out soggy when fried. And so Kroc sent out teams of workers, armed with hydrometers, to make sure all his suppliers were producing potatoes in the optimal solids range of 20 percent to 23 percent.

Preparation and passion. Passion and preparation. Look those words up in the dictionary and you'll see Kroc's picture. Can you envision your picture there?

Do you understand what Kroc did? Do you see why he was able to sell thousands of franchises? Kroc knew the true value of equity, and, unlike Steve from our story, Kroc went to work *on* his business rather than *in* his business. He knew the hamburger wasn't his product—McDonald's was!

So what does *your* real estate investment company need to do to become a little money machine? What is the passion that will drive you to build a company that works—a turnkey system like Ray Kroc's?

Equity and the Turnkey System

What's a turnkey system? And why is it so valuable to you? To better understand it, let's look at another example of a turnkey system that worked to perfection: the recordings of Frank Sinatra.

Frank Sinatra's records were to him as McDonald's restaurants were to Ray Kroc. They were part of a turnkey system that allowed Sinatra to sing to millions of people without having to be there himself.

Sinatra's recordings were a dependable turnkey system that worked predictably, systematically, automatically, and effortlessly to produce the same results every single time—no matter where they were played, and no matter who was listening.

Regardless of where Frank Sinatra was, his records just kept on producing income, profit, flow, and equity, over and over … and still do! Sinatra needed only to produce the prototype recording, and the system did the rest.

Kroc's McDonald's is another prototypical turnkey solution, addressing everything McDonald's needs to do in a basic, systematic way so that anyone properly trained by McDonald's can successfully reproduce the same results.

And this is where you'll realize your equity opportunity: in the way your company does business, in the way your company systematically does what you intend it to do, and in the development of your turnkey system—a system that works even in the hands of ordinary people (and real estate investors less experienced than you) to produce extraordinary results.

Remember:

- If you want to build vast equity in your company, then go to work *on* your company, building it into a business that works every single time.

- Go to work *on* your company to build a totally integrated turnkey system that delivers exactly what you promised every single time.

- Go to work *on* your company to package it and make it stand out from the real estate investment companies you see everywhere else.

Here is the most important idea you will ever hear about your company and what it can potentially provide for you:

The value of your equity is directly proportional to how well your company works. And how well your company works is directly proportional to the effectiveness of the systems you have put into place upon which the operation of your company depends.

Whether money takes the form of income, profit, flow, or equity, the amount of it—and how much of it stays with you—invariably boils down to this. Money, happiness, life—it all depends on how well your company works. Not on your people, not on you, but on the system.

Your company holds the secret to more money. Are you ready to learn how to find it?

Earlier in this chapter, I alerted you to the inevitable conflict between the real estate investor-as-employee and the real estate investor-as-owner. It's a battle between the part of you working in the company and the part of you working on the company. Between the part of you working for income and the part of you working for equity.

Here's how to resolve this conflict:

- Be honest with yourself about whether you're filling *employee* shoes or *owner* shoes.

- As your company's key employee, determine the most effective way to do the job you're doing, *and then document that job.*

- Once you've documented the job, create a strategy for replacing yourself with someone else (another real estate investor) who will then use your documented system exactly as you do.

- Have your new employees manage the newly delegated system. Improve the system by quantifying its effectiveness over time.

- Repeat this process throughout your company wherever you catch yourself acting as employee rather than owner.

- Learn to distinguish between ownership work and employee-ship work every step of the way.

Master these methods, understand the difference between the four kinds of money, develop an interest in how money works in your company . . . and then watch it flow in with the speed and efficiency of a perfectly pounded hammer.

Now let's take another step in our strategic thinking process. Let's look at the subject of *planning*. But first, let's see what Than and Paul have to say about money. ✤

www.michaelegerber.com/co-author

CHAPTER 4

Money and Your Relationship With It

Than Merrill
Paul Esajian

Rich people play the money game to win. Poor people play the money game not to lose.

—T. Harv Eker

We have no doubt that part of what attracted you to real estate in the first place was the potential to earn money—and lots of it. You shouldn't feel bad about that. Embrace it and realize that money is a good thing. It's a measuring stick of the performance of our business and its health. It allows us to take care of our families and, ultimately, it allows us to give back to people and causes we believe in.

The good news is we believe there are very few businesses where ordinary, everyday people can earn the type of income real estate investors can who use "leverage" properly. However, understanding money is more than just knowing how to structure a profitable real estate deal or how to read a balance sheet.

First, you have to understand how investors think about their money and formulate the proper "money mindset." Then you have to figure out what makes real estate unique and how money can be leveraged as an investor. Likewise, you have to determine how money is tracked and flows through your business each month. Finally, you have to understand how to make money on the money that your business produces.

Fixing Your Money Mindset

From years of coaching real estate investors, we realize that some beginners have flawed concepts and viewpoints about money that must be fixed before they can leverage money properly or run a successful business. Some of these concepts are more philosophical in nature and are often reflections of values taught by parents and close family members. Other money concepts we will discuss are specific to the real estate industry. And some are specific to running your own business and the management of your money within the business. So let's take a deeper look.

Wealth begins with a state of mind. If you want to accumulate a great fortune in real estate, you must first believe that you can do it. You can't hope or wish for riches. It must be a keen, pulsating desire, which gets you out of bed in the morning and inspires you into action. This desire must be infinite. Likewise, your belief in your own abilities to accumulate wealth must, at some point, turn into a conviction. You must convince yourself that riches are not beyond your reach, and there is still time to acquire money, fame, recognition, and the happiness you desire. Wealth can be created by anyone who is ready and determined to have these blessings.

It is important to associate and link positive emotions to money and discourage and or eliminate negative emotions. You can come to believe whatever you repeat in your mind—whether that statement is true or false does not matter. If you constantly fill your mind with fear, doubt, and unbelief in your ability to accumulate wealth, your subconscious mind will translate that into its physical equivalent.

Investor vs. Consumer Mindset

As real estate investors, we are in the money business so how we think about money, use money, and leverage it is very different from other businesses. We are not like other professionals who primarily sell their time, services, or widgets. Large amounts of money will flow in and out of your business as you buy and sell properties. So, you must spend more time on changing your mindset about money, because sometimes, even in the very early stages of your business you will have to leverage large amounts of money. This is a good thing, because with leverage comes better returns.

You must learn to think like an investor instead of a consumer. Consumers are fearful of money, fearful of borrowing it, and fearful that their investments will never earn a return. Consumers are always worried about what something costs instead of focusing on what return that investment will make. Consumers are typically very skeptical and make money decisions based on this skepticism.

This mindset exists because many consumers made mistakes with their money in the past. For example, during the real estate refinance boom many consumers pulled equity out of their houses and bought cars, boats, big-screen TVs, etc. Obviously, these assets don't appreciate in value and do not produce a return on investment. In fact, as time passes, these purchases decrease in value, so it's natural to equate all future purchases with this pattern of loss.

Thus, people lose confidence in themselves and their ability to make sound investments with their money. Consumers begin to adopt a scarcity mindset and become negative about money. Oftentimes, they blame outside factors and act very fearful around money.

Investors, on the other hand, think very differently about money and credit. They realize that both money and credit can be leveraged to make even more money. Investors buy assets and make capital investments in their business. They realize that there is a cost to the money they borrow or use, but the return will be much greater. They look at money the way a bank looks at your money. You put your money in the bank and the bank pays you a 1 percent return, for example. The bank then takes that money and leverages it to make a 5 percent return on a home loan or a business loan. Thus, your hard earned money is being leveraged by the bank instead of by you the investor.

In contrast, real estate investors learn how to leverage the banks money by taking out low interest loans and utilizing that money to earn much higher rates of return on their investment deals.

Consumers are very fearful of losing money and protect it at all costs. This fear leads to a rate of return that is often below the inflation rate. Investors understand the power of money and take control of it.

Investors also view themselves and their employees as assets. Thus, astute investors constantly invest in education for themselves and their staff. They realize that the intellectual capital they acquire will produce a much bigger return than the money they invested to acquire it. Investors know that once they learn something, it can never be taken away. A big-screen television loses value every month, but an investment in personal education and development leads to a lifetime of return.

When we coach real estate students, we sometimes have to spend time fixing their mindset about money before we help them make or manage their money.

Leveraging Real Estate

Top surgeons, attorneys, chiropractors, and other high income earners in almost every other profession basically sell time or personal services for money.

In contrast, a real estate investment business is very unique because you can acquire assets using leverage that end up earning income for you on a monthly basis whether you work or not. Let us give you a couple of examples to help you understand this.

We learned about the concept of leverage when we signed a five-year lease for our first business, which was a restaurant. A clause in my lease gave the owner of the building 6 percent of the portion of my gross annual sales that went over our break-even point of $500,000. We remember thinking (after we signed the lease, of course) what a sweet deal this was for the owner.

Most restaurants, when run optimally, operate at a 15 percent profit margin. Simply put, that means 15 cents of every dollar brought in gross sales is considered profit. So in this scenario, *if* (a big if here) we ran my business optimally, we would give 40 percent of my profit to the owner of the building.

Essentially, we were going to trade sixty hours of our time every week to run the restaurant, and the owner of the building was going to leverage our time and share in a large stake of the profits our business generated.

Additionally, our hard-earned money was going to be used to pay down his mortgage and build lifelong equity for him.

Not to mention the fact that we were personally guaranteeing the lease, which meant that the owner of the building could count on a steady stream of income from us for the next five years. Having a five-year lease in place immediately increased the value of the building and the owner's personal real estate holdings.

This wasn't the only area where leverage was being used. When the owner bought the building he financed 80 percent of the purchase with a bank loan. So we were effectively paying down the mortgage on a building that was purchased using borrowed money.

What is even more awesome is that we never met the owner of the building; we only dealt with his property manager. That's what we call a highly leveraged business activity in terms of both money and personal time.

That's when we realized we were in the wrong business.

It was clear that there was significantly more money to be made owning the real estate instead of being the owner of the business leasing the real estate.

Over the years, we continued seeing how this basic principal of leverage makes real estate investors very wealthy. In what other business can you purchase an asset worth a million dollars and only have to put down 20 percent of your own money in order to buy it? When is the last time you saw someone walk into a bank and say, "I would like to borrow $100,000 to buy shares of XYZ stock" and only have to put 20 percent down?

This principal of leverage makes the real estate investing business so uniquely powerful—it's why there is so much more potential for building wealth.

However, understanding this general concept of leverage is only part of the money equation. Next, you need to set very specific goals for how much money you want to earn in your business.

Breaking Down Annual Income

Building wealth, as you know, begins in your mind. The next step is to acquire the specialized knowledge required to succeed in the field of real estate. However, this specialized knowledge alone will not lead to wealth unless it is organized and intelligently directed into a practical plan of action.

As coaches, we always ask our students to set a definite goal of how much they would like to make annually as a real estate investor. Then we examine their market and the niche of real estate they plan on specializing in, so that we can create a plan to back into the number of offers and leads they would have to generate to have the potential of achieving that goal.

For example, let's say the student sets a goal and wants to make $300,000 a year focusing on residential rehab transactions. Typically, we do not advise someone to purchase a property unless they have the potential to earn a 15 percent profit margin or greater. In this hypothetical situation, if the student lives in a market where the median value of a single-family home is $200,000, then we would advise the student to not purchase a property to rehab unless they had the potential of earning a 15 percent ($30,000 or more) on the deal. This is obviously an approximate profit margin assuming the student is working in and around that $200,000 price point on single-family homes, and is running the business optimally.

In this situation, this student would have to do ten deals with this type of profit margin, or just under one deal a month, to achieve his or her annual financial goal. (Yearly profit of $300,000 divided by $30,000 per deal equals 10 deals.) With that number of deals defined, we can help the student approximate how many properties he or she will have to evaluate and make offers on to be able to purchase 10 properties. We have found most investors make about 15 offers to get one deal under contract in the residential arena with a profit margin of 15 percent or greater. In this case, this investor will have to make about 150 offers annually or about 12.5 offers a month, to yield 10 deals a year.

Our goal as coaches is to help students set up their business properly so they can make the appropriate number of offers each month. We then hold students accountable for implementing their marketing campaigns necessary to generate enough leads. Obviously, there are never any guarantees in real estate or any business for that matter. There is risk to manage, skills to develop, and systems that must be implemented. However, it's hard to set and achieve any big, hairy, audacious goal if you can't break it down to what you have to achieve on a weekly and monthly basis.

Creating Monthly and Annual Goals

Once your real estate investment business gets off the ground and you start hiring employees, it becomes vital to set annual revenue goals for the entire investment company. You must then convey those goals to every employee. Divide your annual goal by twelve to set monthly benchmarks and by four to create quarterly ones.

Every quarter, review the goals with everyone in the company. If you hit the number, celebrate with your team. These celebrations help create a team spirit—and your staff will buy into your vision. When you see this team bonding taking place, you should then let the staff know that bonuses or bumps in commission will be tied to these quarterly or annual goals.

Once you create team-wide goals you will be amazed at the transformation that will take place. More offers will get made, rents will be collected on time, invoices will be scrutinized, and longer hours will be worked unasked. More importantly, employees will start paying attention to how their co-workers are using their time and will often show them how to be more efficient. Over the years, setting goals for our team has been *huge!* We experienced a dramatic transformation—and only the strong survived. The weaker members who were holding the team back were forced to change their work habits or were pushed out by our own staff.

Four Kinds of Money

The four kinds of money that Michael discussed in Chapter 3 are very important for real estate investors to understand. They are income, profit, flow, and equity.

Most investors measure their profitability by what they have left in the bank at the end of the month. In other words, whatever you have left over after paying everyone at the end of the month is yours to keep.

We think you need to look at a lot more than your monthly bank statements if you want to properly manage your finances. Every month, you need to make a habit of analyzing your company financials once your bookkeeper has closed out the previous month's books.

Firstly, look at your Profit and Loss statement to see how your business did that month. This will tell you about the first two kinds of money: your income and profit for that month. You should then compare that month to the previous month and every other month in that calendar year.

Ideally, you should compare that number to where you were at the same time last year. It is just a snapshot of your business, but it will tell you a lot about how you are doing month to month and whether your business is growing, stagnant, or declining.

Next, review your company's Balance Sheet and compare it that of the previous month and the previous year. This report is a snapshot of your company's financial health in a year. It lists the current assets, liabilities, and ownership equity. This is where you can track the fourth kind of money: equity.

You also want to look at your cash flow, which Michael simply calls "flow." This is very important for investors to grasp because real estate requires that you make many heavy capital investments when you acquire properties. Over the years, we have tried to minimize the amount of cash we put into deals by borrowing private money or creatively financing properties. But there will be some deals you will have to close on very quickly that will possibly require your own cash. Likewise, the business will require monthly operating capital, so it is important to look at how your money flows through your business every month.

Just by looking at these numbers every month, you will start getting a sense of the flow of money in your business. You can then start to set goals and benchmarks. For example, you may want to have three months' operating expenses in reserve for overhead. Or you may want to have enough reserves to purchase two rehabs paying all cash each year. Or you may want to target 30 percent equity in your business every year. The goals are up to you, but setting them on a monthly and annual basis creates a direction for your business.

Once every quarter or at a minimum every six months, you should also take the time to meet with your certified public accountant (CPA) to discuss the company's health and, more importantly, ways to continue minimizing your tax liability. One of the most crucial lessons we learned in our first year is to not to wait till the end of the year to look at how to reduce tax liability! This is often too late, and the rushed tax planning can lead to bad decision-making. In these meetings with our CPA, we have learned a lot about how to manage our money and maximize the various self-directed retirement vehicles we use to acquire real estate.

Lines of Credit and Private Lenders

There are many sources of capital for your business. We could write a separate book on this topic alone, but for the sake of simplicity, let's limit the discussion to two of the most important sources.

Regardless of what type of real estate you specialize in, you should set up as many business lines of credit for your company as possible. Having a line of credit at a bank is like insurance for business operating capital. It can carry you through a month when cash flow might be at a minimum. It is important that you set one up as soon as possible or before your business needs it. You should only use the line when you absolutely need it. The key is to set it up before you ever need it because banks will be hesitant to extend credit when you are heavily leveraged.

By far the best source of capital for acquiring any type of real estate is private money.

As mentioned in Chapter 2, you typically will pay private lenders a higher return than a traditional bank, but their flexibility and aggressiveness in lending will more than warrant the higher interest rate (of 6 percent to 12 percent). Over the years we have borrowed millions of dollars of private money and have used it for every type of real estate transaction, from residential to commercial.

Loaning your own money as a private lender can be a very lucrative way to invest the profits you make on your real estate deals. This is how we invested the majority of the money we made over the years from flipping properties.

This has been a great way to keep our money working for us. We currently have many loans out on properties that our coaching students are working on. Of course, the deals must be sound and structured correctly if you ever want to invest your own money this way. Over the years we have spent a lot of time teaching other investors how to make safe and secure private mortgage loans on properties and earn incredible rates of return on the money they make in the real estate business.

Equity in Your Business

The last kind of money Michael discussed in the previous chapter is equity. A lot of real estate investors think about equity in terms of equity in the properties they own, but they don't ever think about creating equity in their real estate business as a whole. Consequently, they never consider the natural conclusion of a company, which is the profitable exit or the sale of the business itself. After we read Michael's *E-Myth* many years ago, one of the first things we decided was to design our business to sell.

The true value of your business will be determined by the quality of the systems you develop within the company. Potential buyers of existing real estate businesses will place higher value on how quickly they can plug themselves or their management staff into the business. If your business is completely dependent on your intellectual capital, then there is no value in your business. A potential purchaser can't buy you; they can only buy your systems, the name you have built, and the value of any employees who will remain with the business.

Thinking about how you are going to exit the business is very important. We have helped many people design their real estate businesses so they could sell them. A few students have sold equity in their companies to key employees who wanted to run the business so they could retire or pursue other opportunities. A 10 percent to 51 percent stake in a company that you don't have to spend any time on is a good thing when someone else is doing all the work. A lot of serial entrepreneurs set up their companies like this. They spend a few years building them and then sell part of the ownership to highly qualified managers and earn a portion of the annual income passively. We have sold equity in a couple of business ventures to individuals who then executed a lot of the daily operations of the business. It's a true win-win situation.

Wrapping It Up

For now, take time to reflect on everything we have discussed in this chapter—from the way you think about money, to the investor versus consumer mindset, to specific ways of looking at and managing your money on a monthly and annual basis. It is helpful to dedicate an entire day each month to examining the financial health of your business. This goes way beyond just learning QuickBooks. It's about examining your business's money situation and forecasting for the future.

This is the perfect place to see what Michael has to say about planning. ✤

For more information about how we can help you as a real estate investor go to: www.MasteryForInvestors.com.

CHAPTER

5

On the Subject
of Planning

Michael E. Gerber

Luck is good planning, carefully executed.

—Anonymous

Another obvious oversight revealed in Steve and Peggy's
story was the absence of true planning.
Every real estate investor starting his or her own
company must have a plan. You should never begin to see clients
without a plan in place. But, like Steve, most real estate investors
do exactly that.

A real estate investor lacking a vision is simply someone
who goes to work every day. Someone who is just doing it, doing
it, doing it. Busy, busy, busy. Maybe making money, maybe not.
Maybe getting something out of life, maybe not. Taking chances
without really taking control.

The plan tells anyone who needs to know *how we do things here*.
The plan defines the objective and the process by which you will

45

attain it. The plan encourages you to organize tasks into functions, and then helps people grasp the logic of each of those functions. This in turn permits you to bring new employees up to speed quickly.

There are numerous books and seminars on the subject of company management, but they focus on making you a better real estate investor. I want to teach you something else that you've never been taught before: how to be a manager. It has nothing to do with conventional company management and everything to do with thinking like an entrepreneur.

The Planning Triangle

As we discussed in the Preface, every real estate investor sole proprietorship is a company, every real estate investment business is a company, and every real estate investment enterprise is a company. Yet the difference between the three is extraordinary. Although all three may offer real estate investment services, how they do what they do is completely different.

The trouble with most companies owned by real estate investors is that they are dependent on the real estate investor. That's because they're a sole proprietorship—the smallest, most limited form a company can take. Sole proprietorships are formed around the technician, whether real estate investor or roofer.

You may choose in the beginning to form a company, but you should understand its limitations. The company called a *sole proprietorship* depends on the owner—that is, the real estate investor. The company called a *business* depends on other people plus a system by which that business does what it does. Once your company becomes a business, you can replicate it, turning it into an *enterprise*.

Consider the example of Sea Real Estate Investments. The clients don't come in asking for Douglas Sea, although he is one of the top real estate investors around. After all, he can only handle so many deals a day and be in only one location at a time.

Yet he wants to offer his high-quality services to more people in the community. If he has reliable systems in place—systems that any qualified team member can learn to use—he has created a business and it can be replicated. Douglas can then go on to offer his services—which demand his guidance, not his presence—in a multitude of different settings. He can open dozens of real estate investment companies, none of which need Douglas Sea himself, except in the role of entrepreneur.

Is your real estate investment company going to be a sole proprietorship, a business, or an enterprise? Planning is crucial to answering this all-important question. Whatever you choose to do must be communicated by your plan, which is really three interrelated plans in one. We call it the Planning Triangle, and it looks like this:

- The Business Plan;
- The Deal Plan; and
- The Completion Plan.

The three plans form a triangle, with the business plan at the base, the deal plan in the center, and the completion plan at the apex.

The business plan determines *who* you are (the business), the deal plan determines *what* you do (the specific focus of your real estate investment company), and the completion plan determines *how* you do it (the fulfillment process).

By looking at the Planning Triangle, we see that the three critical plans are interconnected. The connection between them is established by asking the following questions:

1. *Who are we?*—purely a strategic question

2. *What do we do?*—both a strategic and a tactical question

3. *How do we do it?*—both a strategic and a tactical question

Strategic questions shape the vision and destiny of your business, of which your company is only one essential component. Tactical questions turn that vision into reality. Thus, strategic questions provide the foundation for tactical questions, just as the base provides the foundation for the middle and apex of your Planning Triangle.

First ask: What do we do, and how do we do it *strategically?*

And then: What do we do, and how do we do it *practically?*

Let's look at how the three plans will help you develop your company.

The Business Plan

Your business plan will determine what you choose to do in your real estate investment company and the way you choose to do it. Without a business plan, your company can do little more than survive. And even that will take more than a little luck.

Without a business plan, you're treading water in a deep pool with no shore in sight. You're working against the natural flow.

I'm not talking about the traditional business plan that is taught in business schools. No, this business plan reads like a story—the most important story you will ever tell.

Your business plan must clearly describe

- the business you are creating;
- the purpose it will serve;
- the vision it will pursue;
- the process through which you will turn that vision into a reality; and
- the way money will be used to realize your vision.

Build your business plan with *business* language, not *practice* language (the real estate investor's language). Make sure the plan focuses on matters of interest to your lenders and shareholders rather than just your technicians. It should rely on demographics and psychographics to tell you who buys and why; it should also include projections for return on investment and return on equity. Use it to detail both the market and the strategy through which you intend to become a leader in that market, not as a real estate investor but as a business enterprise.

The business plan, though absolutely essential, is only one of three critical plans every real estate investor needs to create and implement. Now let's take a look at the company plan.

The Deal Plan

The deal plan includes everything a real estate investor needs to know, have, and do in order to deliver his or her promise to a client on time, every time.

Every task should prompt you to ask three questions:

1. What do I need to know?
2. What do I need to have?
3. What do I need to do?

What Do I Need to *Know?*

What information do I need to satisfy my promise on time, every time, exactly as promised? In order to recognize what you need to know, you must understand the expectations of others, including your clients, your acquisitions managers, sales people, and other employees. Are you clear on those expectations? Don't make the mistake of assuming you know. Instead, create a need-to-know checklist to make sure you ask all the necessary questions.

A need-to-know checklist might look like this:

- What are the expectations of my clients?
- What are the expectations of my administrators?
- What are the expectations of my team members?
- What are the expectations of my staff?

What Do I Need to *Have?*

This question raises the issue of resources—namely, money, people, and time. If you don't have enough money to finance operations, how can you fulfill those expectations without creating cash-flow problems? If you don't have enough trained people, what happens then? And if you don't have enough time to manage your company, what happens when you can't be in two places at once?

Don't assume that you can get what you need when you need it. Most often, you can't. And even if you can get what you need at the last minute, you'll pay dearly for it.

What Do I Need to *Do?*

The focus here is on actions to be started and finished. What do I need to do to fulfill the expectations of this client on time, every time, exactly as promised? For example, what exactly are the steps to perform when approached by a distressed homeowner who seeks an immediate buyer?

Your clients fall into distinct categories, and those categories make up your business. The best real estate investment companies will invariably focus on fewer and fewer categories as they discover the importance of doing one thing better than anyone else.

Answering the question *What do I need to do?* demands a series of action plans, including

- the objective to be achieved;
- the standards by which you will know that the objective has been achieved;
- the benchmarks you need to reach in order for the objective to be achieved;
- the function/person accountable for the completion of the benchmarks;
- the budget for the completion of each benchmark; and
- the time by which each benchmark must be completed.

Your action plans should become the foundation for the completion plan. And the reason you need completion plans is to ensure that everything you do is not only realistic but can also be managed.

The Completion Plan

If the company plan gives you results and provides you with standards, the completion plan tells you everything you need to know about every benchmark in the deal plan—that is, how you're going to fulfill client expectations on time, every time, as promised. In other words, how you're going to arrange a referral to another investor, conduct routine due diligence on properties, or educate a homeowner about foreclosure options.

The completion plan is essentially the operations manual, providing information about the details of doing tactical work. It is a guide to tell the people responsible for doing that work exactly how to do it.

Every completion plan becomes a part of the knowledge base of your business. No completion plan goes to waste. Every completion plan becomes a kind of textbook that explains to new employees or new associates joining your team how your company operates in a way that distinguishes it from all other real estate investment companies.

To return to an earlier example, the completion plan for making a Big Mac is explicitly described in the *McDonald's Operation Manual*, as is every completion plan needed to run a McDonald's business.

The completion plan for a real estate investor might include the step-by-step details of how to assess the market value of a house after it's fixed up—in contrast to how everyone else has learned to do it. Of course, every real estate investor knows they need to keep expenses lower than the final sales price. They've learned to do it the same way everyone else has learned to do it. But if you are going to stand out as unique in the minds of your clients, employees, and others, you must invent your own way of doing even ordinary things. Most of that value-added perception will come from your communication skills, your listening skills, your innovative skills in transforming an ordinary visit into a great, value-added client experience.

Perhaps you'll decide that a mandatory part of your home-buying procedure with distressed homeowners is to educate them on the options of loan modification, short sale, and foreclosure. If no other real estate investor that your client has seen has taken the time to explain these options, you'll immediately set yourself apart. You must constantly raise the questions: *How do we do it here? How should we do it here?*

The quality of your answers will determine how effectively you distinguish your company from every other real estate investor's company.

Benchmarks

You can measure the movement of your company—from what it is today to what it will be in the future—using business benchmarks. These are the goals you want your business to achieve during its lifetime.

Your benchmarks should include the following:

- Financial benchmarks
- Emotional benchmarks (the impact your company will have on everyone who comes into contact with it)
- Performance benchmarks
- Client benchmarks (Who are they? Why do they come to you? What does your company give them that no one else does?)
- Employee benchmarks (How do you grow people? How do you find people who want to grow? How do you create a school in your company that will teach your people skills they can't learn anywhere else?)

Your business benchmarks will reflect (1) the position your company will hold in the minds and hearts of your clients, employees, and investors; and (2) how you intend to make that position a reality through the systems you develop.

Your benchmarks will describe how your management team will take shape and what systems you will need to develop so that your managers, just like McDonald's managers, will be able to produce the results for which they will be held accountable.

Benefits of the Planning Triangle

By implementing the Planning Triangle, you will discover:

- what your company will look, act, and feel like when it's fully evolved;
- when that's going to happen;
- how much money you will make; and much more.

These, then, are the primary purposes of the three critical plans: (1) to clarify precisely what needs to be done to get what the real estate investor wants from his or her company and life, and (2) to define the specific steps by which it will happen.

First *this* must happen, then *that* must happen. One, two, three. By monitoring your progress, step-by-step, you can determine whether you're on the right track.

That's what planning is all about. It's about creating a standard—a yardstick—against which you will be able to measure your performance.

Failing to create such a standard is like throwing a straw into a hurricane. Who knows where that straw will land?

Have you taken the leap? Have you accepted that the words *business* and *company* are not synonymous? That a sole proprietorship relies on the real estate investor and a business relies on other people plus a system?

Because most real estate investors are control freaks, 99 percent of today's real estate investment companies are sole proprietorships, not businesses.

The result, as a friend of mine says, is that "real estate investors are spending all day stamping out fires when all around them the forest is ablaze. They're out of touch, and that real estate investor better take control of the company before someone else does."

Because real estate investors are never taught to think like businesspeople, the real estate professional is forever at war with the businessperson. This is especially evident in large, multi-location companies, where bureaucrats (businesspeople) often try to control real estate investors (entrepreneurs). They usually end up treating each other as combatants. In fact, the single greatest reason real estate investors become entrepreneurs is to divorce such bureaucrats and to begin to reinvent the real estate investment enterprise.

That's you. Now the divorce is over and a new love affair has begun. You're a real estate investor with a plan! Who wouldn't want to do business with such a person?

Now let's take the next step in our strategic odyssey. Let's take a closer look at the subject of *management*. But before we do, let's find out what Than and Paul have to say about planning. ✤

www.michaelegerber.com/co-author

CHAPTER

6

Having a Plan of Attack

Than Merrill
Paul Esajian

When planning for a year, plant corn. When planning for a decade, plant trees. When planning for life, train and educate people.

— Chinese Proverb

After reading Michael's chapter on planning, you can see how important planning is for any business and the vast opportunity it brings. However, if you are like most real estate investors, you are too busy just doing it, doing it, doing it to dedicate time to planning. If this sounds familiar, then this chapter will really help you.

In real estate, we often get caught up in what we call the "deal-to-deal hamster wheel of death," because this approach is like a death sentence through an unending job in your own business. The sad truth is that the majority of investors we have met over the years do not have any sort of plan for their business, beyond doing more deals and making more money. So let's address this issue and imprint in your mind the importance of planning and the type of strategic planning that needs to be done in a real estate investment business.

We three partners spend a lot of time planning each month in our business and we teach our coaching students to do the same. A lot of our novice students say: "Than, I don't have time to work *on* the business because I am so busy right now. Maybe next month I will get to it." We understand this mindset.

You may already understand some of the basics of how a real estate business operates. You have spent time and money educating yourself on how to do real estate deals and the type of properties you should be and are actively buying. If you are actively buying properties, you understand how profitable the business can be, but you have yet to make serious money because you are still running from deal to deal.

Often, it may seem like the inflow of cash is just above the outflow. You are convinced that your daily schedule does not permit the time to think about planning or working *on* your business. You are too busy searching for deals, evaluating deals, making offers, and trying to sell that house on XYZ Street that just can't find a buyer. Your desk is a mess, and it seems like every day you are putting out fires and only have time to deal with urgent matters. Your to-do list is very long and sometimes you have problems deciding what items you should work on first. Add in family responsibilities and it seems like the "time thief" follows you around like the shadow you didn't know you had.

We can relate to this and feel for you. So let's work on changing these circumstances and discuss your plan of attack as a real estate investor. We've found that regardless of how many pressing matters might be demanding your time, real-world planning must be the engine that guides your business. You can't make educated and timely decisions without having a plan to guide those decisions. In fact, the most important thing you can do every week, month, and year is planning. And you must frequently revisit your plan and continually adapt it to changing market conditions.

We set annual goals, which we break down into projects that we slot into each quarter. We then look at our first quarter's goals and break them down into weekly projects. Every Sunday evening for thirty minutes we determine the course of our week based on that list of weekly projects. We also review the previous week's plan to make sure we are on track to reach our quarterly goals. We have been doing this consistently for years and attribute a lot of our success to this type of planning. We do this for both our personal and business goals.

Learning to Say "No" Unless It's on Your Plan

Steve Jobs, the co-founder of Apple and one of the greatest entrepreneurs in recent times, was asked what the key to his success was. In his answer lies a great lesson:

"Success comes from saying no to 1,000 things to make sure you don't get on the wrong track, or try to do too much. We're always thinking about new markets we could enter, but it's only by saying no that you can concentrate on the things that are really important." —Steve Jobs

We truly believe business success comes not from the opportunities you take, but from the ones you choose not to pursue. Like Jobs, you, as a real estate investor, will have to learn how to say no to a lot of deals and business opportunities.

This is why having a vision and a plan for your business is essential. If you have created a plan and follow it, then it is easier to say no to marginal opportunities that come your way. These are opportunities that distract us as entrepreneurs from our ultimate goal of building a business that is independent of us. This task can be very difficult because all successful entrepreneurs are opportunity chasers on some level. We love the excitement of something new. We often despise the monotony of typical day-to-day business.

Successful entrepreneurs are both dreamers and executors. When we learn about new opportunities, the dreamer within us gets excited because we see a new challenge. Yet this new challenge will undoubtedly require time. Sacrificing time is what stops us from creating systems that automate our existing business.

Having a national TV show, *Flip This House* on A&E, brought this concept to our attention.

Our TV show has been both a blessing and a curse for our business. Obviously, the exposure of being on A&E has been massive, which is great for our business. However, as soon as the show started airing, we got a lot of calls from other business owners, entrepreneurs, and opportunity seekers wanting us to be part of what they called "the next big thing." We seized a few of these opportunities; some definitely added value to our business. However, these occasions were few. The majority of the calls came from what we term serial opportunity seekers, who jump from idea to idea and never follow through on anything. They are always chasing the next big opportunity.

We have jumped at opportunities in our business and poured time into projects only to realize that it did nothing to help grow our core business. Essentially, we were trading time on new things and shifting money from one pocket to the other.

As the phone calls started pouring in, we realized that it was difficult to say no to many of the opportunities that came our way. This was a real problem until we started having monthly meetings where we would discuss our business plans and prioritize our projects. More importantly, we would discuss our execution plans, and often examine other opportunities that came our way. We realized there were a million ways to make money and had no doubt many of the opportunities would be profitable. However, over time, we also realized that the income was small in comparison to what we could make by continuing to focus on our core business.

Later on, we also decided that we would filter all new opportunities so we weren't all evaluating them simultaneously. This made it easier for us and staff to say no to other people. Saying no is very empowering because it tells other people that you have the confidence you need to build the business you want. Not the business other people with their own agenda want you to build. Saying no also sends a strong message to your employees that you have a plan and direction for the business and that you are committed to your vision.

Your Business Plan

Having a business plan is essential. We are not talking about a formal business plan like the one you may have been taught to create in college or business school.

We're referring to a business plan that is related to the direction and vision of the company and the area of real estate you will specialize in. To arrive at this plan, envision the promotional material you would give to a potential buyer or investor in your company who wants to have an overview of your work and know the purpose your business serves in the marketplace. This plan is what we use to communicate to lenders, investors, or people we might partner with on a deal. It includes our buying philosophy, which dictates the types of properties we pursue, the discounts we look for, and our typical exit strategy for each property.

To create this plan, the first thing you have to do is dedicate some time to it. Take a few days with your business partners or by yourself to think about the vision of your real estate business, the purpose it will serve in your life, and how it compares to your original intentions.

Determine Your "Why"

You also want to focus on your "why" as you formulate your business plan. We learned this from a great book written by Simon Sinek called *Start with Why*. Some of the most successful icons of business have one thing in common: they started their own companies and were very clear about their *why*. This clarity enabled them to inspire people to buy into the purpose of the business and achieve remarkable results.

Your *why* is what inspires you to succeed. It is the driving force that motivates you to achieve your goals. It is what keeps your customers loyal to your business instead of going with your competitors. As Sinek points out in his book, people don't buy what you do; they buy why you do it. Most of your competitors can explain what they do; some can explain how they do it, but very few can clearly articulate why they do what they do.

In his book, Sinek uses Apple as an example of a company that has done a great job communicating its why or its corporate vision. That's why Apple's customers are extremely loyal and will literally camp out in line when the company releases a new product.

Apple's employees, as well as its customers, believe in the vision of Steve Jobs. His *why* was to change the world through the products and technology he created, to change the way people do business, to change the way people interact with their computers, and to change the way they think about technology. Look at a company like that and the loyalty it has engendered and compare it to other less-successful companies like Dell or Microsoft. They haven't conveyed the *why* or the vision behind the company as effectively as Jobs has.

If you want to have that customer loyalty and want to become a great manager, you have to define the *why* of your business. You then have to sell your team members on the vision and get them to buy into what you believe.

When you really take the time to discover your *why* and your purpose for doing business, it will inspire you and others around you. Your team and your customers will follow you not because they have to, but because they want to. Essentially, they will adopt your "why" as their own.

Focus on a Niche

Another key item to determine as part of your business plan, as noted in Chapter 2, is the type of properties you are going to focus on. There are many areas of real estate and you can't focus on all. Our most successful coaching students focus on a specialty and rarely deviate from it until they have created systems to automate that niche.

We have also seen investors who start doing deals that then propel them into a specialty. Consider, for example, a student named Chris who specialized in short sale deals and had more than thirty going at one time. During a coaching call, we asked him if he really liked doing short sales. His answer blew us away. He said, "I don't know anything else. The first few deals I got when I started marketing for under-market-value deals were short sales, so that's what I focused on and have been working in ever since."

What happened to Chris is not unique. We see a lot of investors who either get educated about a niche or involved in a niche and they never step back to think if that niche is the best for them and their unique skill sets.

It doesn't matter how you got into a niche of real estate. What matters is your passion for that area of the business; otherwise, you will never maximize your happiness. So, when you are creating your business plan, you have to consider what real estate niche you are going to pursue. It doesn't matter where you are now. If you're a land-lord and you don't really like working with tenants, it's never too late to get into another area of real estate that you have passion for.

Your Completion Plan

The completion plan is by far the most important part of this planning equation. It is your operations manual for how all parts of your business work together. These are your systems.

As Michael teaches, systems are the heart of your business and the engines that drive revenue. Systems are what turn a chaotic and inefficient real estate company into a well-oiled, money-making machine. Systems are what you design and plug other people into so you can free yourself from your business. Simply put, the systems are everything.

If you think it sounds time-consuming or tedious to build systems, try running a business without them. Yes, you may spend a lot of time creating systems, testing them, and tweaking them, but it will pale in comparison to the lifetime of work you will have to do without them.

While building systems in our real estate investing business, we first divided the business into different divisions that each of us was responsible for managing. We created nine divisions, which we still have—no more, no fewer. They are:

1. Marketing
2. Acquisitions
3. Loss Mitigation
4. Financing
5. Construction
6. Sales
7. Property Management
8. Business Management
9. Business Development

We then focused on creating systems for each of the divisions that we individually managed. For example, in the marketing division we looked at all the ways we generated seller and buyer leads, from direct mail to Facebook to filtering through the MLS. Then we documented the marketing execution process for each campaign and set benchmarks for performance. After that, we implemented the system ourselves to make sure we had streamlined its efficiency before handing it off to an employee to execute each week.

In the marketing division, we have eight marketing systems that get executed each month to bring in the leads on properties that we can then make offers on. For each of these systems, we designed a process for weekly and monthly implementation so that we did not have to be involved in any of the marketing campaign work.

The MLS Offer System

One of the ways we find properties is through the Multiple Listing Service. In fact, the majority of properties that sell in most cities around the country are listed and sold through the MLS.

The only issue is that with the sheer number of properties that will be listed each year you must have a good system to filter through the MLS to find the deals that have potential.

Thus, we created what we call our MLS offer system to help us filter through the sheer number of properties that are listed on the MLS to find the deals that have the highest profit potential. As I give you an overview of how this system works, I believe you will begin to understand the full scope of what a system looks like. You will also begin to see how every system requires technical work, managerial work, and entrepreneurial work.

The majority of the technical work is done by our acquisitions team members who work in our real estate office and filter through the newly listed properties that hit the MLS every day. Individuals on our acquisitions team then reach out to the listing agents to gather further information about the properties we are interested in. After they gather the information we then perform the rest of our due diligence which includes everything from running comparable sales to actually going out to the property to estimate repairs.

Our acquisition manager (*manager*) is responsible for evaluating the research so that a verbal or written offer can be formulated and presented to the listing agent. These offers are based on a preset acquisition formula. We know the majority of these offers will be rejected by the sellers, but success is a numbers game. Our system calls for making 30 offers a week to yield two deals per week.

Our MLS offer system is divided into three sub-systems, related to each step of the process: Find, Research, and Offer.

Find

Under this sub-system, our acquisitions team searches for newly listed MLS properties twice a day. That is because deals listed on the MLS are highly competitive, in contrast to other strategies we use to find deals. Every real estate agent has access to every listed property on the MLS, so their investor clients will compete with us on listed properties. Thus, we make speed itself a competitive advantage.

For example, in our target area, between 50 and 150 properties typically hit the market every day. Of those properties, only 10 percent to 15 percent will have what we consider true investor potential and will need to be researched further. Most listed properties are what we would consider "retail" listings and aren't good for investment purposes, because they are priced for the consumer market. Retail houses are purchased by people who want to live in them and do not seek a profit margin.

Instead, we focus on the remaining 10 percent to 15 percent of properties that have the potential for higher profit margins like preforeclosures, bank owned (REOs), probate properties, and other types of distressed properties. We also like it when the property remarks indicate that the listing agent is open to working with investors who make lower offers.

In our system, we have instructed our acquisitions team to search the MLS for real estate agent remarks that use words like: fixer, must sell, cracked slab, TLC, contractor, gut, work, motivated, quick close, cash, handy. Our technicians also search for special financing remarks like: 203k, Homepath, Homestep, Fannie Mae, renovation financing. This helps narrow down the properties that have the most potential.

Research

The next sub-system in the MLS offer system is research. Once we find a potential property, we contact the listing agent to see how much activity the property has had and whether the seller is open to offers from investors. If we find that the agent is focused on retail buyers, then the property will fall low on our priority list. If the agent is open to working with investors and realizes the benefits an investor brings to the table, then we will move it to our "property pursuits

d we generally send an offer within forty-eight hours.

Fundamental to this sub-system's success is how quickly and accurately the research is done. Once a property hits our "property pursuits list," we run comparables on the property to determine the after-repair value of the property. Then, one of our the members on our acquisitions team will drive to the property to estimate repairs and to verify the after-repair value of the property. Seeing the property helps us determine its as-is value, estimated repair costs, and after-repair value—how much it could sell for once it's fixed up.

Offer

Once a property makes it through the first two sub-systems, it goes to the last one. At this step, we make an offer. This is either making a verbal offer to the listing agent or having the listing agent write the offer for us to sign. If the offer is negotiated or accepted, we go to contract. If the offer is rejected, we indicate in our database to "follow up" and resubmit the same offer after thirty, sixty, and ninety days, if the property is still on the market. A lot of our deals come from aggressively following up on properties where the seller had previously rejected our offer.

As you can see, the MLS offer system contains three smaller systems, which each comprise several steps. The key is to document everything so that anyone you hire to do technical or managerial work can duplicate your actions. These small steps add up to sub-systems, which add up to larger systems that help you reach your business goals.

In true E-Myth fashion, you will have to wear all the hats when you are starting out. But as you develop systems and work *on* your business, rather than *in* your business, you will quickly replace yourself in each role. As you progress up the ladder from *technician* to *manager* to *entrepreneur*, you will begin to free yourself from your business.

The MLS offer system example shows the approach you need to take in all areas of your business. This approach has transformed our business, from tasks as simple as answering the phone to running major construction projects. We build every division in our real estate business the same way. Our acquisitions division has six systems managed by our acquisitions manager. Our construction division has seven systems managed by our project manager. Our sales system has four systems managed by our sales manager.

These systems took years to create, refine, and test. In fact, during the first three years of our business, we focused two days a week purely on building systems and looking for ways to create step-by-step business processes. We made this activity a priority, so we could eventually leverage our time effectively and build a business that did not depend on us. These are the systems we now pass on to our coaching students, so they do not have to reinvent the wheel.

Nobody Does It as Good as I Do

You might think that nobody can do the same job that you do. Sometimes you are correct, at least initially, until you hire talented people and train them on your system. Often they will do it better than you. In fact, even if they perform at 60 percent of your capacity, they will likely generate a lot more revenue for the company than the salary you pay them. Plus, if you don't replace yourself, then you will never free yourself from the business.

Your systems and completion plan ensure that those who replace you know exactly what to do, what is expected of them, and how you measure their performance. It also ensures that if they leave, you can easily put someone else into that role and not skip a beat. Employee turnover is one of the biggest costs for a business and that is why it is important to have set, structured business processes and systems. You never want your company to experience a setback when a key person decides to leave.

When you develop systems that are easy to follow, your employees will feel much more confident about what they do, which will ultimately lead to a higher level of profitability.

Wrapping It Up

Once you have completed the planning process, you have to start putting your plan into action, which will require that you develop your management skills. So let's continue on our transformational journey and learn how to manage the people who will help you implement your plan.

As you will see in the next chapter, Michael has many insights to share about management. ✤

For more information about how we can help you as a real estate investor go to: www.MasteryForInvestors.com.

CHAPTER

7

On the Subject of Management

Michael E. Gerber

Good management consists of showing average people how to do the work of superior people.

—John D. Rockefeller

Every real estate investor, including Steve Walsh from our story, eventually faces the issues of management. Most face it badly.

Why do so many real estate investors suffer from a kind of paralysis when it comes to dealing with management? Why are so few able to get their real estate investment company to work the way they want it to and to run it on time? Why are their managers (if they have any) seemingly so inept?

There are two main problems. First, the real estate investor usually abdicates accountability for management by hiring an office manager. Thus, the real estate investor is working hand in glove with someone who is supposed to do the managing. But the real estate investor is unmanageable himself!

71

The real estate investor doesn't think like a manager because he doesn't think he is a manager. He's a real estate investor! He rules the roost. And so he gets the office manager to take care of stuff like scheduling appointments, keeping his calendar, collecting receivables, hiring/firing, and much more.

Second, no matter who does the managing, they usually have a completely dysfunctional idea of what it means to manage. They're trying to manage people, contrary to what is needed.

We often hear that a good manager must be a "people person." Someone who loves to nourish, figure out, support, care for, teach, baby, monitor, mentor, direct, track, motivate, and, if all else fails, threaten or beat up her people.

Don't believe it. Management has far less to do with people than you've been led to believe.

In fact, despite the claims of every management book written by management gurus (who have seldom managed anything), no one—with the exception of a few bloodthirsty tyrants—has ever learned how to manage people.

And the reason is simple: *People are almost impossible to manage.*

Yes, it's true. People are unmanageable. They're inconsistent, unpredictable, unchangeable, unrepentant, irrepressible, and generally impossible.

Doesn't knowing this make you feel better? Now you understand why you've had all those problems! Do you feel the relief, the heavy stone lifted from your chest?

The time has come to fully understand what management is really all about. Rather than managing *people*, management is really all about managing a *process*, a step-by-step way of doing things, which, combined with other processes, becomes a system. For example:

- The process for on-time scheduling
- The process for answering the telephone
- The process for greeting a client
- The process for organizing client files

Thus, a process is the step-by-step way of doing something over time. Considered as a whole, these processes are a system:

- The on-time scheduling system
- The telephone answering system
- The client greeting system
- The file organization system

Instead of managing people, then, the truly effective manager has been taught a system for managing a process through which people get things done.

More precisely, managers and their people, *together*, manage the processes—the systems—that comprise your business. Management is less about *who* gets things done in your business than about *how* things get done.

In fact, great managers are not fascinated with people, but with how things get done through people. Great managers are masters at figuring out how to get things done effectively and efficiently through people using extraordinary systems.

Great managers constantly ask key questions, such as:

- What is the result we intend to produce?
- Are we producing that result every single time?
- If we're not producing that result every single time, why not?
- If we are producing that result every single time, how could we produce even better results?
- Do we lack a system? If so, what would that system look like if we were to create it?
- If we have a system, why aren't we using it?

And so forth.

In short, a great manager can leave the office fully assured that it will run at least as well as it does when he or she is physically in the room.

Great managers are those who use a great management system. A system that shouts, "This is *how* we manage here." Not "This is *who* manages here."

In a truly effective company, how you manage is always more important than who manages. Provided a system is in place, how you manage is transferable, whereas who manages isn't. *How* you manage can be taught, whereas *who* manages can't be.

When a company is dependent on *who* manages—Katie, Kim, or Kevin—that business is in serious jeopardy. Because when Katie, Kim, or Kevin leaves, that business has to start over again. What an enormous waste of time and resources!

Even worse, when a company is dependent on *who* manages, you can bet all the managers in that business are doing their own thing. What could be more unproductive than ten managers who each manage in a unique way? How in the world could you possibly manage those managers?

The answer is: You can't. Because it takes you right back to trying to manage *people* again.

And, as I hope you now know, that's impossible.

In this chapter, I often refer to managers in the plural. I know that most real estate investors only have one manager—the office manager. And so you may be thinking that a management system isn't so important in a small real estate investment company. After all, the office manager does whatever an office manager does (and thank God, because you don't want to do it).

But if your company is ever going to turn into the business it could become, and if that business is ever going to turn into the enterprise of your dreams, then the questions you ask about how the office manager manages your affairs are critical ones. Because until you come to grips with your dual role as owner and key employee, and the relationship your manager has to those two roles, your company/business/enterprise will never realize its potential. Thus the need for a management system.

Management System

What, then, is a management system?

The E-Myth says that a management system is the method by which every manager innovates, quantifies, orchestrates, and then monitors the systems through which your company produces the results you expect.

According to the E-Myth, a manager's job is simple: A *manager's job is to invent the systems through which the owner's vision is consistently and faithfully manifested at the operating level of the business.*

Which brings us right back to the purpose of your business and the need for an entrepreneurial vision.

Are you beginning to see what I'm trying to share with you? That your business is one single thing? And that all the subjects we're discussing here—money, planning, management, and so on—are all about doing one thing well?

That one thing is the one thing your company is intended to do: distinguish your real estate investment business from all others.

It is the manager's role to make certain it all fits. And it's your role as entrepreneur to make sure your manager knows what the business is supposed to look, act, and feel like when it's finally done. As clearly as you know how, you must convey to your manager what you know to be true—your vision, your picture of the business when it's finally done. In this way, your vision is translated into your manager's marching orders every day he or she reports to work.

Unless that vision is embraced by your manager, you and your people will suffer from the tyranny of routine. And your business will suffer from it, too.

Now let's move on to *people*. Because, as we know, it's people who are causing all our problems. But before we do, let's see what Than and Paul have to say about management. ❦

www.michaelegerber.com/co-author

Becoming a Manager

Than Merrill
Paul Esajian

The productivity of work is not the responsibility of the worker but of the manager.

—Peter F. Drucker

Real estate investing is a team sport and you are only as strong as the team you surround yourself with. Unfortunately, we had to learn this lesson the hard way in our first year of doing business. A "whale" of a deal came in through one of our direct mail pieces. Since our business was new, this deal was significantly more profitable than all the other projects we had completed. Naturally, we acted with a sense of urgency and went to meet with the seller and look at the project in less than an hour after taking the call.

The home was in a luxurious area and the seller was willing to sell the home for significantly below its worth if we could close quickly. The seller was getting divorced and wanted to move to Florida.

Knowing all these things we figured the quickest way to solve her problems was to buy the home "subject to" the existing debt. We knew if we bought the home "subject to" and left the existing mortgage in place that we could close within a few days because we wouldn't have to raise money from a private lender to finance the deal.

We offered to purchase the property "subject to" the mortgage just above what the seller owed. She was fine with the price, but because of her unfamiliarity with the "subject to" deals, she wanted her attorney to review the offer. That afternoon we called her attorney to present the deal, but the attorney wanted to only deal through our attorney. So within minutes of leaving the seller's house we called our attorney. We presented the terms of the deal so he could put the deal together with the other attorney. Our attorney assured us it wouldn't be a problem and that he would call the other attorney that afternoon.

The next day, we called our attorney, but got his voice mail and were forced to leave a message. The day after that, we called our attorney again and left a second voice-mail message. The following day we realized we better call the seller to let her know our attorney hadn't called us back yet. She said our attorney never called her attorney and that she had signed a contract with another investor.

Even though we didn't get the deal we did learn a very valuable lesson about the importance of making sure you have a great team that understands your sense of urgency and respects your business enough to get things done immediately. It was a very difficult lesson to learn, but one that allowed us to make some important changes in our team.

The lesson we want to pass on to you is very simple. You can only go as far as your team goes. If you don't choose the best team members to work with then your business will suffer. If you do take the time to interview and find the best team members, put the right systems into place, and learn how to manage and motivate them, then your business will prosper.

Build Yourself Out of Your Business

If your goal is to build a business that is not dependent on you, then you must have a high-quality team and pay them accordingly. It is your job as the business owner to find the most talented people who are available at the pay scale the position warrants. Finding and recruiting A-level talent is your most important job as the driver of the business.

Who are the members of your team and how do you manage them so they achieve optimal performance for your business? This requires management skills, which we discuss in this chapter.

Your real estate team can be divided into two major categories:

1. *External team.* This consists of any outside real estate professional who is involved in a real estate transaction.
2. *Internal team.* This consists of people who work directly for you.

External Team

Your external team is made up of real estate professionals who are involved in your transactions. These external team members affect the profitability and speed of your deals. They also determine how much personal time you have to put into each deal. External team members include real estate agents, mortgage brokers, hard money lenders, insurance agents, a title company and/or an attorney (depending on the state you live in and the closing process in that state), and contractors.

These professionals don't work for you, but with you. They have their own businesses, but they are very integral in closing your real estate transactions, so you have to find the best people, based on statistics if possible. Every real estate transaction is unique and the closing process will sometimes involve very few parties and sometimes it will involve multiple parties depending on how you are acquiring or selling the property. That's why it is so important to have control of as much of the deal as possible utilizing the services of the real estate professionals you work with on a consistent basis. Having control means you will have fewer deals that blow up in your face.

That's why you don't want to work just from referrals or from job posting sites to find members of your external team. You want to work with the best, not your cousin's friend Bruno, who happens to be a licensed real estate agent and also owns a tattoo shop down the street. Bruno is not going to make your life easy when it comes to closing your deals.

In all seriousness, let's discuss the roles and responsibilities of a few of these key professionals, how they help your business, and exactly how to find the best in the business, so you can sip piña coladas in the Bahamas while deals are getting closed by your team.

Real Estate Agents

Having a few good real estate agents as part of your team is essential to your businesses success. You will want to work with both relatively new agents, who will do some of your research on potential properties you will be making offers on, as well as experienced agents with whom you will establish relationships for referral deals and buyers.

First, there is a ton of research that has to be done on properties you plan to make offers on, especially if you are getting a high percentage of your deals from the new MLS listings every day. This is why you want to have at least three to four good buyers agents you can train in your systems to research properties, run sales comparables, view properties, take pictures, and make simple property repair lists.

We spend about forty-five minutes to an hour researching each property before making an offer. If you don't have a streamlined system, your agents might take four to five hours researching each property, which is why a lot of investors burn through their agents very quickly.

The buyers agents, or field agents as we call them, who work for us know that a lot of our offers don't get accepted. Usually, it's about one out of fifteen offers so there is a lot of research that goes into deals that never generate a commission for them. This is why you will most likely end up working with relatively new agents who have not built up a referral basis of business and are hungry to work with investors like you. This is also why we felt it was critical to streamline the process and create a system for our agents so they can be as efficient as possible.

Second, it is critical to also establish relationships with a few of the top producing real estate agents in your area. Top producers are the agents who get the majority of listings from banks and private sellers based on their relationships and years of experience. Top producers also have the biggest pool of potential buyers for your properties. Once you have a relationship with one of these agents, they often will let you know about a potential deal before it ever gets listed. So let's discuss how to score a couple of top producers for your team.

All real estate agents are required to input their listings into the local MLS when they sign a listing agreement with a seller. Thus, all listing volume is tracked within the MLS database and by the local board of real estate agents. To identify the top producing agents, all you have to do is find a real estate agent who knows how to run listing statistical reports within their MLS database based on closed listing volume for the past year. Note that some MLS databases will let you search for this data.

The best place to start is by asking a real estate agent you know (who actually knows the MLS inside and out) if they can research and determine who the top twenty producing agents are, based on closed listing sales. It's a good idea to be present when the agent is doing this research because it is important to look at what types of listings these agents primarily focus on. Ideally, you want to work with agents who get a lot of their listings from banks and distressed sellers.

Once you have identified who the top producing agents are, you should take the time to call and or go to lunch with each one of them. It's not essential, nor will it be possible that you will establish a relationship with every single one. You are only looking for a few long-term relationships that will lead to future deals. All the other agents should know who you are, though, and have an idea of your role in the market. This is essential if you want to create a dominant presence in an area.

It's key to establish how you can be of benefit to that agent in the near future. We let all agents know that we are just one tool they can rely on in their tool box. We do this by letting agents know that many of our offers will be lower than other retail clients they might find, but for hard-to-sell properties or those requiring the bank or seller to move quickly, then that's where we come in. Likewise, we let the agents know that if they have properties that won't qualify for traditional financing based on the current condition of the property, then we are a good fit. There are a lot of benefits to working with investors and all you're trying to do is establish how serious of a buyer you are, how well financed you are, and the fact that you could result in multiple commissions annually.

Remember, you will be submitting many offers to these agents over the course of the next few years, so you must put a face to your business and at least have some sort of relationship, even if it is casual at best.

It should be noted that there is a definite benefit to being an agent yourself when you are trying to establish these relationships. Real estate agents trust and prefer working with other agents for many reasons. Over the years we have found it highly advantageous to be licensed and that's why we opened our own brokerage. We have students who have started investment brokerages under us as well.

Our real estate brokerage is another income stream for us, and it can be for your business as well. We believe the two businesses complement each other perfectly, especially when you're actively marketing for motivated sellers. That's because a lot of sellers who respond to your marketing will not be motivated enough to sell to you at the discount rate you need as an investor, but the property is still a great listing. So if you have the appetite for it, we highly encourage you to get your license.

Mortgage Brokers

When you're selling properties that you have rehabbed, you will need a good mortgage broker to work with who can get your retail buyers financed. Ideally, you want someone who has a large client base and very good mortgage-processing systems. Banks are cautious about whom they lend to; that's why you need a mortgage broker who knows how to get things done quickly and has relationships with the underwriters.

Ideally, you want to work with one of the top mortgage brokers in the area who is consistently closing a lot of loans with a wide variety of loan products. You can find them through referrals from real estate agents, title companies, or real estate investment clubs. Generally speaking, your mortgage broker has to have very good telephone communication skills and the ability to close the client on working with them. It is not essential, but beneficial if they are local because they can also meet in person with clients you refer them who need that personal touch.

You will be sending to your mortgage broker potential buyers who have contacted you or have seen one of your properties. Many times they are looking at your house and a few others so it's essential when you refer them to your mortgage broker that not only does the broker work quickly, but he also knows how to position your properties so the potential buyers end up purchasing one from you.

One other thing that is very important is that your mortgage broker knows the nature of your business and that often you are buying properties and reselling them for considerably more within a three-month time frame. Many banks will "red flag" a loan on a property that was bought for considerably less and is being sold for a lot more within a very short time period. That's why it is very important to document everything you did to improve the property from a construction standpoint so that this information can be relayed to the mortgage broker who is in contact with the bank underwriter.

The bottom line is you don't want to lose a deal because the buyer's financing fell through. Your mortgage broker will help ensure that buyers of your property qualify to close—so you can get paid.

Hard Money Lenders

Hard money lenders are niche lenders who finance properties that most banks traditionally won't lend on. In contrast to private lenders, these are professional lenders, including many who are former rehabbers who will take the property and finish the job if you fail to repay your loan. In exchange, they charge much higher interest rates and points, and have loan terms that are usually six to twelve months. Typically, most hard money lenders charge between 12 percent and 18 percent and two to five points (one point is 1 percent of the loan amount) to borrow their money.

In contrast to banks, hard money lenders will also typically fund the construction costs a property requires. This portion of funding is taken in draws against work that is being performed. If you're thinking this is expensive in comparison to what banks usually charge, you are correct. However, a lot of banks won't lend on residential properties that need considerable work unless you apply for a special loan product that has much stricter lending criteria.

Remember, as an investor it's not so much about the cost of money, but the availability that is important. You have to calculate the cost of money into the profitability of the deal and if it is still a highly profitable deal then often it will make sense to borrow money even at higher interest rates. Banks have a role in what we do as investors, but we very rarely use them for residential properties we have to purchase quickly, fix up, and sell. You also have a competitive advantage in a market when you can close quickly on properties.

Over the years we have financed a lot of our projects utilizing hard money lenders. We also referred a lot of our wholesale buyers to hard money lenders to get financing. These wholesaler buyers buy our contracts, then do the rehab job. And our relationships with hard money lenders have also benefited us in other ways. Many of them have referred buyers to us who ended up purchasing properties from us.

Whether you utilize their money or not, you can see the many benefits of having a few good relationships with hard money lenders in your area. Such lenders are also very easy to find, especially by doing a Google search for lenders with experience loaning in the areas you have targeted to buy. Typically, there will not be more than a handful; some can't be identified because they don't advertise.

Insurance Agents

One of the easier team members to find will be a good insurance agent. You can ask real estate agents, mortgage brokers, and other investors for referrals. The key is to choose an insurance agent who understands that you will be buying properties that need significant work. The insurance policies you get will be very different from the ones traditional homeowners get because many of the properties you buy may not have working mechanicals, and may have structural issues and sometimes even cracked foundations.

Title Agent/Attorney

Depending on which states you are buying and selling in, you will need a good escrow company, title company, and/or closing attorney. Different states handle real estate closings in different ways so you will want to find out the standard procedure in the state you are going to do the most business in. Either way, it is important that you have an open line of communication with whoever is handling your closing and they understand the nature of your business.

As investors we purchase properties using creative financing techniques, like owner financing or "subject to" the existing mortgage, so the party handling your closing needs to understand the structure of these closings. Likewise, many of the properties we sell would have been owned for a very short period of time so your title agent or attorney must understand the structure of your transactions.

The key is to find an escrow agent or attorney who does a lot of closings with other experienced investors in your area. If you close in a state that traditionally utilizes attorneys to handle real estate closings, it is very important to make sure you work with an attorney who specializes in this form of law. Attorneys can have many different specialties so just because a law firm does real estate closings doesn't mean it specializes in them. So do your due diligence to find a firm where at least half of the work or more is related to real estate.

As you can see, you will have to find and develop relationships with many external team members. When you have built a quality team of professionals, your life will be a lot easier because they will handle a lot of your transactional work so you can focus on other areas of the business. Now, let's switch gears and discuss your internal team.

Internal Team

Your internal team consists of employees you hire directly to fill a specific position as your business grows. The employee makeup of your office will differ based on the type of real estate deals you focus on.

Here is a look at the positions in our office:

- Personal assistant: does admin and mundane tasks, so you can focus on more strategic activities
- Office manager: runs the day-to-day operations of the office
- Acquisitions manager: manages the process of evaluating leads and making offers
- Project manager: manages construction projects

- Short sale manager: handles files on short sales
- Sales manager: a good agent or an in-house sales manager who sells properties
- Property manager: manages the properties we buy and hold
- Bookkeeper: handles all the bookkeeping
- Interns: handle the grunt work
- Real estate agents: licensed brokers who help you buy and sell your properties

All these people have a defined role in our company. The exact structure and order in which you hire for these positions will differ based on the types of properties you target and your individual skill set. Some of our coaching students with very profitable and successful businesses have smaller teams than ours, while other students have very large teams because they work on a volume basis.

What is more important than knowing the individual roles is having a system for developing your management skills. To achieve that, we've developed a five-step system. These steps are: self-accountability, business vision, business systems, the right people, and training.

1. Self-Accountability

Realize that *you* are usually the Number 1 problem in your business. When we talk to real estate investors and examine their business as a consultant or coach, we hear them complain about the people they have hired. They may have hired the wrong people. However, most of the time, the fault lies with the business owners themselves. They don't have a sound employee-hiring system so they can't find the right people. They don't have a system to train their employees and they haven't documented all the steps necessary in that particular position to perform at a high level. Having no systems or direction is a recipe for disaster.

We were the problem in our own business when we started; in fact, we knew nothing about how to manage and work with other people. We were highly motivated and had acquired a great deal of knowledge about real estate, but we had no idea how to manage and run a business. So, the first thing you have to do is have a level of self-accountability and a desire to study what it takes to be an excellent manager. Managers are not born, they are developed.

2. Business Vision

You need to determine a vision for your business. What you're doing is discovering your *why*, as we discussed in Chapter 6. What is your purpose for being in business, what is your cause, what do you believe in? If you don't have a *why* or you don't have a purpose for your business, then what can other team members or employees buy into?

We would argue that most business owners have no greater purpose than just making money. If you want your business to be remarkable, you have to determine what your *why* is and communicate this to your team members, employees, and your customers.

Our vision for our company is social change. We do a lot of things with nonprofit organizations and socioeconomically challenged families. We give back to the community in that way. Another why is social change within our team members themselves. We believe in developing the minds of our team members and letting them prosper beyond their jobs, beyond just working and earning a paycheck.

Keeping your own *why* in mind is very important when you're hiring somebody and explaining your vision. Everything becomes easier once you've done that.

3. Business Systems

You have to have systems for every position in your business. A system essentially creates a formal structure for a common business process. Depending on the complexity of a business, it may be made up of hundreds of individual systems. It becomes very difficult to manage someone without having established systems, goals, and expectations.

In our acquisitions department, we have six systems to analyze and put deals under contract. One system we automated was how to properly take a lead from a seller, what questions to ask, what information we need to know, how we create and build rapport with the seller, and how to schedule an appointment on a deal that looks promising. This system is now executed every single day, multiple times a day, by our acquisitions team.

This system then is connected to a second one within the acquisitions department where we value the property the customer is looking to sell. Depending on the property type, we take various steps to determine the current market value, as well as the after-repair value. We talk more about these processes in later chapters.

The acquisitions department also leverages our company database, customer relationship management (CRM) system—which tracks everything from name and numbers to e-mail exchanges and personal information about clients (discussed in more detail in Chapter 20)—the MLS, and other tools and software to store all our critical information about the properties we analyze. The deal leaves acquisitions as soon as we have closed on the property.

Essentially, the systems that make up the acquisitions department allow us to evaluate hundreds of properties a month. We narrow that number down and end up buying ten to fifteen properties. The same type of setup, in which systems drive business processes, exists in and between all our departments.

4. The Right People

Most businesses look at a very small talent pool and sometimes end up choosing the lesser of all evils. For example, if you are only using Craiglist.com to find job applicants you are limited to the pool of talent that is specifically looking for a job on that website.

When you are looking for talent, you have to cast a very wide net. To do this you should spend ample time and leverage multiple employment websites. You also should develop a referral network of other business owners who are well networked and might have leads on talented potential employees. The wider the talent pool you consider, the better-quality people you're going to find.

We look for people who have the right personality traits and attributes over experience. Experience is valuable; we definitely take that into consideration, but people's personality must fit our company culture.

Ideally you want someone who thinks and acts like an entrepreneur within your business. We call this person an "intrepreneur." You don't want someone who only wants to work 9 to 5. You should look for the best possible person in the pay scale you offer for the position. If you are hiring an assistant manager, you are not going to get a CEO, but if you are paying $15 an hour for an assistant, you want to get the most talented and self-starting person available at that pay rate.

You have to realize that hiring the right people is essential if you ever want to sell your real estate business. Your management team, and what we call your "bench strength," is vitally important. When people look at buying your business, they will examine the quality of your management team because you're not going be around. So you want to design your business as if you were going to sell it this year, by finding the right people to work in it.

5. Training

Once you find the right people, you've got to train them and let them prosper. We will discuss this in detail a little later in the book, but we mention it now because you must develop your basic management skills before you start hiring people.

You should also document everything you do and begin to create a training system for your future growth. Ongoing training is essential for all employees if you want to grow your business. At our company, we created an online training center. Using a software program called Camtasia, we recorded position-specific training videos for every area of the business. The videos are housed on a password-protected blog for new hires to review. We talk more about this in Chapter 24.

As the owner, you also want to invest in your own training. We ourselves have attended dozens of business and personal seminars to maximize our performance and effectiveness. For example, you might learn to let your employees make their own mistakes and learn from them. You can't micromanage or expect everything to be perfect. Perfectionism, a lot of times, is like a disease. People micromanage their new hires because they feel like they can do the work better themselves. That may be true, but you can't grow without employees, because your own time is obviously limited.

Here's how we got over our micromanagement disease. Initially, we were doing all the property acquisitions at our business. We thought about training someone to take over the role, but it made us nervous. What if the person did not have or develop all of the necessary skills? What if the person could only do the job 80 percent as well as we could? Then we thought, what if we had two people performing at 80 percent of our capacity? After all, we would make more money as a company as long as the pay structure was set up correctly, because we would have two individuals performing at a relatively high level, as opposed to just ourselves.

You can't work and grow other areas of the company if you're involved in every single aspect of the business. So you have to train people properly. That means you have to create a training system. The most important thing is to let employees take ownership of that training system and improve it. As soon as people take ownership of the system and believe it's *theirs*, their productivity will increase. You could easily impose a system upon employees, but that doesn't get them to buy in. Let them play an active role in tweaking the system and tailoring it to their work. Encourage them to ask questions and come up with ideas.

When you manage this process properly, you will be pleasantly surprised. Your employees will develop and modify your system and make it better. That's why finding the right people and training them is so important. Train them, let them prosper, and then get the heck out of the way.

Wrapping It Up

Our five-step management system—self-accountability, business vision, business systems, the right people, and training—provides a basis to help you develop your skills as a manager and prepare your business for future growth. Remember, you can only go as far as the team in which you build. So build intelligently.

Now, let's take a look at what Michael teaches us about people in the next chapter. ❧

For more information about how we can help you as a real estate investor go to: www.MasteryForInvestors.com.

On the Subject of People

Michael E. Gerber

*Very few people go to the doctor when they have a cold. They go to the
theatre instead.*

—Oscar Wilde

E very real estate investor I've ever met has complained
about people.

About employees: "They come in late, they go home
early, they have the focus of an antique camera!"

About mortgage lenders: "They're living in a non-parallel universe!"

About clients: "They want to buy a mansion on a town-
home budget!"

People, people, people. Every real estate investor's nemesis. And
at the heart of it all are the people who work for you.

"By the time I tell them how to do it, I could have done it twenty
times myself!" "How come nobody listens to what I say?" "Why is it
nobody ever does what I ask them to do?" Does this sound like you?

So what's the problem with people? To answer that, think back to the last time you walked into a real estate investor's office. What did you see in the people's faces?

Most people working in real estate investing are harried. You can see it in their expressions. They're negative. They're bad-spirited. They're humorless. And with good reason. After all, they're surrounded by people who lost their homes, can't qualify for a loan, lost their jobs, or can't get their offers accepted. Clients are looking for nurturing, for empathy, for care. And many are either terrified or depressed. They don't want to be there.

Is it any wonder employees at most real estate investment companies are disgruntled? They're surrounded by unhappy people all day. They're answering the same questions 24/7. And most of the time, the real estate investor has no time for them. He or she is too busy leading a dysfunctional life.

Working with people brings great joy—and monumental frustration. And so it is with real estate investors and their people. But why? And what can we do about it?

Let's look at the typical real estate investor—who this person is and isn't.

Most real estate investors are unprepared to use other people to get results. Not because they can't find people, but because they are fixated on getting the results themselves. In other words, most real estate investors are not the businesspeople they need to be, but *technicians suffering from an entrepreneurial seizure.*

Am I talking about you? What were you doing before you became an entrepreneur?

Were you a corporate executive working for a large multi-location organization? A midsized company? A small company?

Didn't you imagine owning your own company as the way out?

Didn't you think that because you knew how to do the technical work—because you knew so much about rehab management, research and acquisitions, sales screening, and property management—that you were automatically prepared to create a company that does that type of work?

Didn't you figure that by creating your own company, you could dump the boss once and for all? How else to get rid of that impossible person, the one driving you crazy, the one who never let you do your own thing, the one who was the main reason you decided to take the leap into a business of your own in the first place?

Didn't you start your own company so that you could become your own boss?

And didn't you imagine that once you became your own boss, you would be free to do whatever you wanted to do—and to take home *all* the money?

Honestly, isn't that what you imagined? So you went into business for yourself and immediately dived into work.

Doing it, doing it, doing it.

Busy, busy, busy.

Until one day you realized (or maybe not) that you were doing all of the work. You were doing everything you knew how to do, plus a lot more you knew nothing about. Building sweat equity, you thought.

In reality, a technician suffering from an entrepreneurial seizure.

You were just hoping to make a buck in your own company. And sometimes you did earn a wage. But other times you didn't. You were the one signing the checks, all right, but they went to other people.

Does this sound familiar? Is it driving you crazy?

Well, relax, because we're going to show you the right way to do it this time.

Read carefully. Be mindful of the moment. You are about to learn the secret you've been waiting for all your working life.

The People Law

It's critical to know this about the working life of real estate investors who own their own real estate investment company: *Without people, you don't own a company, you own a job.* And it can be the worst job in the world because you're working for a lunatic! (Nothing personal—but we've got to face facts.)

Let me state what every real estate investor knows: Without people, you're going to have to do it all yourself. Without human help, you're doomed to try to do too much. This isn't a breakthrough idea, but it's amazing how many real estate investors ignore the truth. They end up knocking themselves out, ten to twelve hours a day. They try to do more, but less actually gets done.

The load can double you over and leave you panting. In addition to the work you're used to doing, you may also have to do the books. And the organizing. And the filing. You'll have to do the planning and the scheduling. When you own your own company, the daily minutiae are never-ceasing—as I'm sure you've found out. Like painting the Golden Gate Bridge, it's endless. Which puts it beyond the realm of human possibility. Until you discover how to get it done by somebody else, it will continue on and on until you're a burned-out husk.

But with others helping you, things will start to drastically improve. If, that is, you truly understand how to engage people in the work you need them to do. When you learn how to do that, when you learn how to replace yourself with other people—people trained in your system—then your company can really begin to grow. Only then will you begin to experience true freedom yourself.

What typically happens is that real estate investors, knowing they need help answering the phone, filing, and so on, go out and find people who can do these things. Once they delegate these duties, however, they rarely spend any time with the employee. Deep down they feel it's not important *how* these things get done; it's only important that they get done.

They fail to grasp the requirement for a system that makes people their greatest asset rather than their greatest liability. A system so reliable that if Chris dropped dead tomorrow, Leslie could do exactly what Chris did. That's where the People Law comes in.

The People Law says that each time you add a new person to your company using an intelligent (turnkey) system that works, you expand your reach. And you can expand your reach almost infinitely! People allow you to be everywhere you want to be simultaneously, without actually having to be there in the flesh.

People are to a real estate investor what a record was to Frank Sinatra. A Sinatra record could be (and still is) played in a million places at the same time, regardless of where Frank was. And every record sale produced royalties for Sinatra (or his estate).

With the help of other people, Sinatra created a quality recording that faithfully replicated his unique talents, then made sure it was marketed and distributed, and the revenue managed.

Your people can do the same thing for you. All you need to do is to create a "recording"—a system—of your unique talents, your special way of practicing real estate investment, and then replicate it, market it, distribute it, and manage the revenue.

Isn't that what successful businesspeople do? Make a "recording" of their most effective ways of doing business? In this way, they provide a turnkey solution to their clients' problems. A system solution that really works.

Doesn't your company offer the same potential for you that records did for Sinatra (and now for his heirs)? The ability to produce income without having to go to work every day?

Isn't that what your people could be for you? The means by which your system for practicing real estate investing could be faithfully replicated?

But first you've got to have a system. You have to create a unique way of doing business that you can teach to your people, that you can manage faithfully, and that you can replicate consistently, just like McDonald's.

Because without such a system, without such a "recording," without a unique way of doing business that really works, all you're left with is people doing their own thing. And that is almost always a recipe for chaos. Rather than guaranteeing consistency, it encourages mistake after mistake after mistake.

And isn't that how the problem started in the first place? People doing whatever they perceived *they* needed to do, regardless of what you wanted? People left to their own devices, with no regard for the costs of their behavior? The costs to you?

In other words, people without a system.

Can you imagine what would have happened to Frank Sinatra if he had followed that example? If every one of his recordings had been done differently? Imagine a million different versions of "My Way." It's unthinkable.

Would you buy a record like that? What if Frank were having a bad day? What if he had a sore throat?

Please hear this: The People Law is unforgiving. Without a systematic way of doing business, people are more often a liability than an asset. Unless you prepare, you'll find out too late which ones are which.

The People Law says that without a specific system for doing business; without a specific system for recruiting, hiring, and training your people to use that system; and without a specific system for managing and improving your systems, your company will always be a crapshoot.

Do you want to roll the dice with your company at stake? Unfortunately, that is what most real estate investors are doing.

The People Law also says that you can't effectively delegate your responsibilities unless you have something specific to delegate. And that something specific is a way of doing business that works!

Sinatra is gone, but his voice lives on. And someone is still counting his royalties. That's because Sinatra had a system that worked.

Do you? Now, we will move on to the subject of team members. But before that, let's see what Than and Paul have to say about advisors. ✤

www.michaelegerber.com/co-author

CHAPTER

10

Your
Advisory Team

Than Merrill
Paul Esajian

It's not always what you know . . . it's who you know.

—Anonymous

A s a former NFL player (albeit with a very short career), Than
has always believed in the power of coaching. In fact, we
would say eight of the ten most influential people in our lives
were coaches of some sort. These coaches influenced our actions,
bettered our decisions, and ultimately shaped us in a way that has
resonated through all areas of our lives.

As real estate investors and small-business owners, we highly
recommend you find people who can coach you as well. You likely
will not find one individual who has the skills to coach you in every
area of your business, so you should seek out and build a complete
advisory team. The people you choose as advisors and the depth of
the relationship you develop with them will ultimately affect the
growth of your business.

As we discussed in Chapter 8, your real estate business is composed of internal and external team members. Internal team members are people who work for you, such as employees. External team members are professionals and associates, such as real estate agents and mortgage brokers, who are involved in different aspects of your real estate deals.

There are two other key groups of people though, who are just as essential to your business success: (1) coaches and mentors, and (2) mastermind peer groups. This chapter focuses on how to develop relationships with these groups of people. Think of your advisory team like a corporate board of directors who will help you brainstorm, develop, and make many key decisions along the way.

Coaches and Mentors

Becoming an entrepreneurial real estate investor is something many of your friends and family will admire you for. Not many people have the self-discipline it takes to venture out on their own and hang their own shingle. When you own your own business, what you accomplish each and every day is up to you. You won't necessarily have someone looking over your shoulder and holding you accountable for daily progress like when you work for someone else. Consequently, it will be lonely at times and time itself can be the enemy.

As an athlete I always appreciated having a coach who would not only push me, but also help guide me strategically to set and achieve my goals. I always wanted to put myself in the best position to succeed in the shortest amount of time, and that's why coaching was so important to me. In business, it's also very helpful to have a coach or someone who can advise you and hold you accountable to the goals you set for yourself.

In my athletic career I realized that my coaches could see what I wasn't able to see about my personal development and performance. With a few choice insights and practice sessions they brought my game to another level.

For example, when I was drafted by the Tampa Bay Buccaneers, my defensive backs coach was a man called Mike Tomlin. In the first two weeks of practice, with Mike's guidance, I learned more about the strategy of the game of football than I had in my previous ten years of playing the sport. Mike showed me how, even though I didn't have top speed, I could still compete at a high level by having a superior understanding of how to read an offense. By implementing what Mike taught me, I was able to raise the level of my performance so I could compete with the other players who often had superior athleticism. Mike has since gone on to become a Super Bowl-winning head coach of the Pittsburgh Steelers.

Through athletics I also realized that coaches can change the way you think. They have a plan for your development that ultimately could not be realized without them. Having the opportunity to be coached by greats like Tomlin, Dick Jauron, and Tony Dungy, I realized that they had a "proven method" for developing younger players into future stars. In fact, many of the players they coached over the years have become stars in the NFL. Likewise, a few of the players they have coached have also been inducted into the NFL Hall of Fame. In business, it is no different.

For example, the majority of Fortune 500 CEOs, men and women who lead the largest and most successful companies in the world, get corporate and business coaching. Many of these individuals are the highest earners on the planet and many of them attribute their success to being open-minded about learning, continually developing their management skills, and coaching.

Unfortunately, some misguided people think it's a weakness if they need to get coaching. Often, this is simply because they let their egos or other people's perceptions of them get in the way of their true success. You know the type: those who never stop to ask for directions as they spend an extra hour and a half trying to get to a destination that's thirty minutes away. Can you imagine the owner of an NFL team deciding to go without coaches one year to save money? Obviously, that's absurd and would never happen. Yet, that is the exact choice some real estate investors make when they decide to start their businesses.

Years ago, we realized that in real estate it is impossible to know everything there is to know. In our first year of business, we made a lot of bad decisions based on a lack of experience. These decisions were costing us thousands of dollars and enormous amounts of time. That's why we made a commitment to finding a team of coaches who could advise us in different areas of the business.

It was actually a relief once this team was assembled, because we realized we didn't have to know it all. We just had to continue developing and rely on the decision-making advice of our expert team of advisors. In a sense, this was another form of intellectual leverage, because we could call on them anytime to lend us their "deal" and business experience.

In fact, before we picked a focus there would often be days where we were working simultaneously in many different sectors of real estate in a single day. Can you imagine in one day working on a wholesale deal on a single-family home, while at the same time trying to analyze two different apartment deals and all the while fielding calls from contractors on twenty ongoing rehab projects? We felt like the proverbial octopus on roller skates. The only way we could stop the madness was to take a step back, slow down, and spend time in finding and establishing our board of advisors. We told each other we had to assemble our coaching staff, so we did. We even tried to field a cheerleading team, but that didn't work so well.

In all seriousness, here are the important players on our team:

Marketing Mentor

Learning how to market successfully is not something that came naturally to us. We also didn't realize early on just how important it is to have consistent marketing in bringing in deal flow. After our first rehab project, which took six months to complete and sell, it took us two months to find our next deal, because we had zero marketing activities. Our office conditions were so poor we could hear crickets chirping inside. That's when we decided to find coaches who could teach us to market ourselves on something other than Match.com.

We ended up going to many seminars on marketing, both offline and online, and we found two mentors who were very successful marketers and helped us grow our business immediately. We realized that marketing was the lifeblood of our business and it didn't matter how much we knew about real estate if we didn't have any deals to analyze and make offers on.

We realized that you need to build a brand presence for your business to generate referral investor leads and have at least three to four direct response marketing campaigns to generate seller and buyer leads each month. If your whole business is dependent on one marketing channel then you have a very high-risk business. Marketing response rates change as competitors enter and leave the market, lists you buy change, and marketing costs change, so you never want your whole business dependent on one marketing channel. We'll talk more about this in Chapter 16.

Negotiation and Sales Mentor

They say in life you don't get what you want—you get what you negotiate. When we first got into the field of real estate investing we didn't realize how much negotiation could affect the profitability of a deal.

There are literally tens of thousands of dollars at stake on an average $200,000 property. That is not even taking into consideration the price you pay for the property, which is obviously the most critical negotiation. When you buy a property you can negotiate everything from the real estate agent's commission to the closing costs to the points and interest you pay on the financing you get from a private or hard money lender. Obviously, your construction budget is completely negotiable with the contractors that you hire. When you sell the property, everything is negotiable from the commissions to the closing costs on the sell side of the transaction.

Likewise, your sales and communication skills are essential skills that need to be developed. When we started buying and selling houses we didn't have a clue about what it takes to communicate and sell at a high level. We realized we needed to study how to sell because we had never held a position where sales skills were required. Over the years we have created relationships with some of the best sales trainers and mentors in the country and have attended many seminars on the subject.

We have paid many of these trainers and coaches tens of thousands of dollars to come train us and our entire office. In real estate, you are constantly selling yourself whether you are working with an agent, contractor, seller, or buyer. It is an essential skill and craft that you should take a serious interest in developing. You will see immediate strides in your business when you continue developing your communication and sales skills.

Remember, we are not born salespeople pitching products on QVC. Nor do we know the many approaches and traits that master negotiators use in their day-to-day life. That's why it's essential for you to find other people who have mastered the craft and learn from them.

Business Management Mentor

Buying and selling real estate and understanding the mechanics of how real estate deals are done is one thing. Learning how to run, grow, and scale a business is something completely different.

We say this because our first year in business was a nightmare. We literally worked the entire year without a day off because we were so focused on doing deals. The only problem is that every other area of our lives was suffering. We almost got out of business at that point, even though we were making good money. The problem was that our business *owned* our time and us. We were literally the "red-headed step-child" of our own real estate business. We thought more time could fix our problems, but unfortunately that wasn't the case.

So we got a real estate business coach, who began to identify and see problems that needed to be fixed. He had a different way of looking at things from the outside in and immediately we began making huge strides. The first thing we fixed was how we spent our time on a day-to-day basis. We started to outsource many of the mundane marketing activities that were consuming our time. Upon our coach's advice, we also implemented and built a back-end database to track all our contacts, leads, offers, and transactions. This saved massive amounts of time every day. We also started really tracking the financials of our business, which resulted in additional profit well over six figures the same year.

Much like my athletic coaches, our business coach was leading us on a set path that resulted in more "time freedom" from our business.

Legal Mentor

Naively, we thought very early on that we could use one attorney for all our real estate-related matters. We quickly realized this is not the case.

Attorneys usually have a specialty. We now have various legal specialists who advise us on everything from business law to contract law to employment law to handling evictions to planning and zoning law to litigation to, finally and most importantly, our legal and asset-protection structures.

You need specialists who can give you the best advice that can literally save your business from disaster, because Murphy is probably one of your tenants who will flush a potato down the toilet and flood all three of your townhouse units. We are not joking. We had a tenant who was using the toilet as a garbage disposal, but that's a whole other story.

Tax Mentor

Whether you like it or not, you have a partner on every single real estate transaction. Your partner is the Internal Revenue Services.

It goes without saying that taxes are a good thing except when you are paying them. As mentioned before, we learned that we needed a tax specialist on our team after our first full year of business, which is also when it was too late to do any advance tax planning. Our tax bill was enormous and we remember thinking, how the heck are we going to pay that? A lot of our profits were tied up in other deals.

Luckily, we were able to pay the tax bill without incurring any interest and that was a very valuable lesson on why we needed to find a tax specialist. Little did we know that there are some very easy ways to reduce and defer your tax liability when you are buying and selling real estate.

And no, getting tax advice from your Uncle Larry who owns his own pizza joint and likes to hide the dough is probably not the best idea.

We highly recommend you find and start building relationships with all these kinds of strategic advisors. Remember, you don't have to know it all—you just have to assemble a team of people who know it all. It may take you some time to find the right people, but keep asking other investors, networking, and testing, until you find the right fit for your team.

Mastermind Groups

Paul is a highly skeptical person. He is the type of guy who always thinks the glass is half empty. I, on the other hand, have always believed that the glass was half full and could use some more water. When I decided to invest a significant amount of money in a mastermind group that met only twice a year, Paul was skeptical.

However, we both realized after participating in that group that it was one of the best decisions we ever made as business owners. In that first mastermind group and numerous others we have joined since then, we created some of the best business relationships with some of the brightest real estate investors in the country.

A mastermind group is very different from having coaches. A good mastermind group is usually made up of peers in your industry who are trying to achieve very similar things with their own businesses. It is a group of people you can brainstorm with and share best industry practices. The collective genius of the people within the group is what makes it so valuable. In any group there will be people with a wide variety of backgrounds and experiences who can provide creative insight for your ideas.

Ideally, in the mastermind group you want real estate investors who live and do business in other markets of the country. They will be more open about best practices than investors in your area who are potential competitors. Ideally, you get together with these individuals a couple times a year, so that you can continue to build and foster the relationships within the group. One relationship or one idea is all it takes to make a mastermind group worthwhile, no matter the investment. There is always something that other people in the room are better at than you.

Ideally, you want a mastermind group that has a set agenda and a wide variety of people with different business experiences. Likewise, there should be a culture of openness within the group so that everyone can participate.

Wrapping It Up

Over the years, seeking out and building a team of strategic advisors has been why we have been able to grow our business so quickly. Likewise, the mastermind groups we have been part of spurred ideas for other seven-figure real estate-related businesses.

We are also very proud to say that this community of individuals working together to achieve a common goal is a service that we have provided to our Mastery coaching students. We have helped more than a thousand individuals launch their real estate businesses.

Now let's dive into another important topic and discover what Michael has to say about team members. ✤

For more information about how we can help you as a real estate-investor go to: www.MasteryForInvestors.com.

On the Subject of Team Members

Michael E. Gerber

Associate yourself with men of good quality if you esteem your own reputation, for 'tis better to be alone than in bad company.

—George Washington

I f you're a sole practitioner—that is, you're selling only your-self—then your real estate investment company called a *sole proprietorship* will never make the leap to a real estate investment company called a *business*. The progression from sole proprietorship to business to enterprise demands that you hire other real estate investors to do what you do (or don't do). Contractors call these people subcontractors; for our purposes, we'll refer to them as team members.

Contractors know that subs can be a huge problem. It's no less true for real estate investors. Until you face this special business problem, your company will never become a business, and your business will certainly never become an enterprise.

Long ago, God said, "Let there be real estate investors. And so they never forget who they are in my creation, let them be damned forever to hire people exactly like themselves." Enter the associates.

Solving the Team Member Problem

Let's say you're about to hire a team member. Someone who has specific skills: carpentry, mortgage broking, seller's agent, whatever. It all starts with choosing the right personnel. After all, these are people to whom you are delegating your responsibility and for whose behavior you are completely liable. Do you really want to leave that choice to chance? Are you that much of a gambler? I doubt it.

If you've never worked with your new associate, how do you really know he or she is skilled? For that matter, what does "skilled" mean?

For you to make an intelligent decision about this team member, you must have a working definition of the word *skilled*. Your challenge is to know *exactly* what your expectations are, then to make sure your other real estate investors operate with precisely the same expectations. Failure here almost assures a breakdown in your relationship.

I want you to write the following on a piece of paper: "By *skilled*, I mean . . . " Once you create your personal definition, it will become a standard for you and your company, for your clients, and for your team members.

A standard, according to *Merriam-Webster's Collegiate Dictionary, Eleventh Edition,* is something "set up and established by authority as a rule for the measure of quantity, weight, extent, value, or quality."

Thus, your goal is to establish a measure of quality control, a standard of skill, which you will apply to all your team members. More important, you are also setting a standard for the performance of your company.

By creating standards for your selection of other real estate investors—standards of skill, performance, integrity, financial stability, and experience—you have begun the powerful process of building a company that can operate exactly as you expect it to.

By carefully thinking about exactly what to expect, you have already begun to improve your company.

In this enlightened state, you will see the selection of your associates as an opportunity to define what you (1) intend to provide for your clients, (2) expect from your employees, and (3) demand for your life.

Powerful stuff, isn't it? Are you up to it? Are you ready to feel your rising power?

Don't rest on your laurels just yet. Defining those standards is only the first step you need to take. The second step is to create a *team member development system.*

A team member development system is an action plan designed to tell you what you are looking for in an associate. It includes the exact benchmarks, accountabilities, timing of fulfillment, and budget you will assign to the process of looking for team members, identifying them, recruiting them, interviewing them, training them, managing their work, auditing their performance, compensating them, reviewing them regularly, and terminating or rewarding them for their performance.

All of these things must be documented—actually *written down*—if they're going to make any difference to you, your team members, your managers, or your bank account!

And then you've got to persist with that system, come hell or high water. Just as Ray Kroc did. Just as Walt Disney did. Just as Sam Walton did.

This leads us to our next topic of discussion: the subject of *estimating.* But first, let's find out what Than and Paul have to say on the subject of employees. ❖

www.michaelegerber.com/co-author

CHAPTER 12

Hiring and Training Employees

Than Merrill
Paul Esajian

Train everyone lavishly. You can't overspend on training.

—Thomas Peters

One of the best things about running your own business is that you can create a community of people you enjoy spending time with. Some of the people who work with us are now our closest friends, with whom we spend much of our time in and out of the office. We literally created our own community of like-minded individuals who all believe we are building something greater than ourselves.

As I have previously shared, athletics were a big part of my personal background. Some of my happiest memories in my life haven't been the games we won or the personal awards—they were the friendships I made and the life experiences I shared with my teammates. I believe we all seek to be connected and understood, and much of our lives will be spent working, so we might as well enjoy that time by creating an environment that others enjoy as well.

That doesn't mean you should hire your college friend just because he makes you laugh. At the end of the day, your business still has to make a profit and there are many people out there who will be a good fit for your business and push you to even higher levels.

In our business, we put a priority on recruiting talented people who fit in our culture. As the owner of your business, you will want to do the same thing. One of your highest and best uses as the head of your team is to create positions that generate revenue and find the most talented people to fill those positions.

In our real estate business, we've created an eight-step employee-growth system for hiring and training employees:

1. Evaluate the existing system
2. Outline the position
3. Define personality traits
4. Thoroughly screen candidates
5. Train and let your team prosper
6. Develop their "intrepreneurial" skills
7. Give your team autonomy
8. Move your team to commission

Evaluate the Existing System

Whenever we used to get overwhelmed, one of our natural reactions was to think we needed to hire someone to offset our personal workload. After years of thinking this way, we can assure you this is not always the best solution. Sometimes it's the system itself that needs to be made more efficient so you can drastically reduce the time it takes to perform that same activity.

For example, we used to spend over ten hours a week putting together direct mail campaigns to motivated sellers. We are talking about mailing lists, mail merges, and literally licking, sticking, and stuffing envelopes. We seriously used to feel high after licking over five hundred envelopes in a single sitting. But no worries; like President Bill Clinton, we never inhaled.

After months of doing this, we decided it probably wasn't the best use of our time. So we decided to hire someone else to "solve" our time problems. For two years, we managed a team of two people who executed our direct mail campaigns. This was an easy and immediate answer, but looking back it wasn't the best or the most efficient answer. We now outsource all our direct mail to a direct mail fulfillment house that actually costs us less money and time to manage each month. What used to take us ten hours of work a week takes our marketing manager about fifteen to twenty minutes a month.

So when you think you have a position that needs to be filled, you should first do an analysis of the effectiveness of the system itself to see if you really do need someone or if the system needs fixing. Along the same lines, you could have a very disorganized team member who tells you he needs help because he is overworked. First, you should help him evaluate the system before you hire someone who may not be necessary.

Either way, when you or your team member goes through the system evaluation you will inevitably make improvements. Many times we have found better technology or a process that can save hours of work by taking a different approach. You might determine that you don't need someone full time in your office and that you only need to hire a virtual assistant for a few hours a week once the system is improved. We have found that a combination of outsourcing certain time-consuming projects and streamlining tasks has eliminated the need to hire a full-time person.

We have seen many real estate companies over-hire, resulting in a lot of confusion and extra overhead. As a business owner, you should do what we do—sit down with the team member who feels overwhelmed and evaluate her work and processes together. The goal is to see if there is a way to make that team member more efficient so that you can keep your new hires to a minimum and do it only when it's absolutely necessary.

Unfortunately, you will sometimes find that you need to replace a staff member as you evaluate the system or a bottleneck in the system. You may learn that you have a B-player in a role that needs an A-player. Sometimes, an A-player in that position might be able to do all the work and eliminate the need for a second hire.

Outline the Position

Once you have determined you need help to avoid collapsing from overwork, it's time to start outlining the work responsibilities of your new hire.

The first thing you need to determine, especially if you're a new business owner, is what that person will take off your plate. Freeing up your time so you can focus on being more strategic is always important, especially with your first few hires. You then want to create a mind map (visual outline) that outlines his or her responsibilities each week and the systems he or she will work with or manage.

Then, determine whom this new team member will report to every week and what business metrics are of value to you. For example, our acquisitions manager reports every week on the number of properties evaluated, offers made, and properties that went to contract that week. He also reports all other deals in contract and how close they are to closing. Ideally, you create weekly goals that reset every week because that will give your team members something to strive for.

For administrative positions, you want to make sure you have what we call "default jobs." They are tasks to be executed if everything gets accomplished in a day, so that your team members are always getting things done and making progress.

The next thing to determine is how the new position will drive revenue for your business. The pay range you're going to offer will be your investment, and you will want to make a return that is at least three times the investment. For example, if you're paying someone $50,000 a year, you want the position to produce at least $150,000 a year in revenue.

Of course, some organizational positions don't directly drive revenue. You can't always come up with a statistic for the revenue, but what you're looking for, at that point, is how the person will save you time as a business owner or how the person will help others to be more strategic with their time and thus drive revenue. So if you're hiring somebody who will process real estate transactions, consider this: Will it make your acquisitions manager more efficient and, therefore, bring in more deals?

When we define a position—long before we start interviewing— we look at the pay for that position and, more specifically, at how that position could move to commission at some point down the road. We discuss this in detail later on in this chapter.

Define Personality Traits

Certain positions require particular personality traits. If you're hiring a processor for all your real estate closings, you will need somebody who is extremely organized and has good communication skills.

As a business owner, you should always try to hire people who have skill sets that you and your other team members don't have. We call this "1+ hiring." If you're a great communicator, a visionary, and an entrepreneur, but you're a bit disorganized, your office manager doesn't have to possess the skills you have, just the ones that will offset those you lack.

You might want to consider having job applicants take a basic personality test to get an idea of who you will be working with.

Thoroughly Screen Candidates

We never understood how important this next step was until we read an awesome book written by Brad Smart called *Top Grading*. After reading it, we realized all the mistakes we were making during our interviews and why we had made a few bad hires in our first years of building a business.

The *Top Grading* process is the holy grail of interviewing, if there is such a thing. It dramatically decreases your probability of making a bad hire, which can be very costly for your business. The interview process is lengthy and often consists of multiple interviews that can last three to four hours. However, it also ensures that you find the best possible people at the pay scale you are offering.

You will uncover everything you need to know about a potential candidate because of the thoroughness of the interviews. You will spend a lot of time covering everything from work history to personality traits to personal competencies.

While interviewing, we evaluate prospects' problem-solving skills by asking them to resolve the kinds of problems and business situations that we have encountered in the past. That way, we can evaluate their level of thinking and their entrepreneurial skills.

We then go through a very thorough executive summary and candidate scorecard to rank the candidates. This process gives us an apples-to-apples comparison and ensures that we hire an A-player. In a pinch, you might hire a friend or your spouse on a part-time basis. That usually works out for the best in our company. Ask us how we know!

Train and Let Your Team Prosper

We are always impressed by how being around other smart people in our company pushes us to get better each day. We have always believed in hiring talented people and then giving them every resource we can afford to let them prosper.

Consequently, we have also met and coached other investors who were "nervous" about training their employees, because they thought they were training their possible future competition. It is a normal fear. However, we have learned over the years that it's better to offer the best possible training to your team even at the risk of them leaving you. We believe that your business will suffer more if you don't train your team members right, and you will actually have a greater chance of people jumping ship if you constantly constrain their personal growth.

That being said, either way you definitely will want to create a very thorough training system for new employees to undergo in the first thirty days on the job. During this process, schedule meetings once or twice a week where employees can get their questions answered. Make sure your training is adequate so that people know what is expected of them and aren't awaiting instruction from you.

When your team members don't know what to do, often it is because the business owner didn't provide clear instructions. If you have hired the right people, they will take your training system and run with it. If, after the initial training, your new hire is still asking you multiple questions every hour, either your training system needs to be improved or you possibly hired the wrong person, or both.

It is very important to note that you should have some flexibility in the systems you create so that your team members can make adaptations to them and take personal ownership. For example, one year we set a goal to purchase more short sale properties. The problem was each individual deal was taking us too long to negotiate and process using our existing system.

So instead of sitting down and improving the system myself, we held a brainstorming session with two of our acquisitions team members and let them come up with ideas about how the system and process could be improved. After about two hours of listing various ideas, we decided they were better suited to improve the system over the next month. All we needed to do was facilitate the brainstorm meetings and provide structure to what they were doing and they could execute the solutions.

At the end of the month, they had created a brilliant process and were 100 percent committed to making sure it succeeded. We know that if we had done the work ourselves and then just demanded they switch over to the new system we created, we definitely would not have gotten the same amount of productivity. It was a very valuable lesson that we continue to utilize in a lot of areas of our business today.

Develop Their 'Intrepreneurial' Skills

Once you have a team member up and running who is productive, we highly recommend you give her a little time each week to develop her "intrepreneurial" skills. An "intrepreneur," as we said before, is a worker who takes an entrepreneur's approach in an existing business. So she develops her own ideas that generate revenue and boost the business's bottom line. At the same time, your team members will enjoy the time they get each week to work the creative side of their brains.

We recommend giving people set time during the week to work on projects that are not necessarily related to their day-to-day tasks. So for 10 percent to 20 percent of their time, allow them to be creative, to work on any area of the business they want, where they feel they can make a drastic improvement. This enables them to add value to your business, many times in ways you've never thought of. It also gets them excited about what they do. A person who is excited to work will produce dramatically more revenue than someone who's just punching a clock.

Give Your Team Autonomy

Autonomy is essential to an A-player. If you can give team members autonomy, flexibility, and decision-making responsibilities, they will *love* working for you.

Depending on the job, give employees the option, if possible, to work from home on certain days of the week. If you've selected the right people, you can trust them to do their work well. With autonomy, their productivity will dramatically increase. As long as your team members are hitting their metrics, give them the freedom to grow and also to be creative. Make sure you have a system to evaluate employee production and, if needed, check on what they're doing.

Employee autonomy is directly linked to the level of overall work satisfaction, and a satisfied worker leads to overall stability and profitability in the business.

Move Your Team to Commission

One thing we have learned from working with really talented people in our own company is that top performers want to perform and be pushed. They also want to be rewarded at times for the extra revenue they produce, which is completely understandable.

A lot of times people can earn more if they are given a commission structure that has been well thought-out. When you move employees to commission status, it allows them to earn more and it creates a lower overhead for you, as the business owner. Your employees won't feel as limited income-wise and will have the incentive to work harder to increase their earnings. A lot of positions in a real estate business can be moved to commission.

When you set up a commission structure, be sure to let employees know that it may change based on how many other people you hire and how the business grows. Not all positions can be moved to commission, but it's in your best interest to do so if it's possible. Employees will have a bigger upside, get more out of their job, and you will have less risk and cost. Commissions allow people to grow and not feel stifled by the parameters of their position.

For really key people, you can set up an employee profit-sharing plan, a 401(k) program, or another long-term savings plan so that they feel invested in the business. With these plans, you allow employees to grow and add value to the business while simultaneously incentivizing them to stay with you for a longer period of time. You don't want your best people to leave, because they're an asset to your business. As you grow, you always want your best people to remain and prosper with your business. So, make it worth their while to continue working for you.

Wrapping It Up

In the past few chapters, we've devoted a lot of attention to how to find, interview, and train employees—a process that's vital to the success of your real estate investing business. The quality and capacity of your team will directly determine how profitable you are and how much happiness the business will bring them and you. Now let's find out what Michael has to say about estimating fees. ✤

For more information about how we can help you as a real estate investor go to: www.MasteryForInvestors.com.

CHAPTER

13

On the Subject of Estimating

Michael E. Gerber

The best we can do is size up the chances, calculate the risks involved, estimate our ability to deal with them, and then make our plans with confidence.

—Henry Ford

One of the greatest weaknesses of real estate investors is accurately estimating how long a rehab job will take and then scheduling their sales accordingly. *Webster's Eleventh* defines estimate as "a rough or approximate calculation." Anyone who has visited a housing renovation site knows that those estimates can be rough indeed.

Do you want to see someone who gives you a rough approximation? What if your real estate investor gave you a rough approximation on the value of a property you are interested in?

The fact is that we can predict many things we don't typically predict. For example, there are ways to assess the market value of house. Look at the steps of the process. Most of the things you do are standard, so develop a step-by-step system and stick to it.

In my book *The E-Myth Manager*, I raised eyebrows by suggesting that doctors eliminate the waiting room. Why? You don't need it if you're always on time. The same goes for a real estate investment company. If you're always on time, then your clients don't have to wait.

What if a real estate investor made this promise: on time, every time, as promised. "Impossible!" real estate investors cry. "Each client is different. We simply can't know how long each appointment will take."

Do you follow this? Since real estate investors believe they're incapable of knowing how to organize their time, they build a company based on lack of knowing and lack of control. They build a company based on estimates.

I once had a real estate investor ask me, "What happens when a distressed homeowner contacts us to sell his house, and we discover that its foundation needed to be repaired? How can we deal with that so unexpectedly?" My first thought was that it's not being dealt with now. Few real estate investors are able to give generously of their time. Ask anyone who's been to a real estate investor's office lately. It's chaos.

The solution is interest, attention, analysis. Try detailing what you do at the beginning of an interaction, what you do in the middle, and what you do at the end. How long does each take? In the absence of such detailed, quantified standards, everything ends up being an estimate, and a poor estimate at that.

However, a company organized around a system, with adequate staff to run it, has time for proper attention. It's built right into the system.

Too many real estate investors have grown accustomed to thinking in terms of estimates without thinking about what the term really means. Is it any wonder many real estate investment companies are in trouble?

Enlightened real estate investors, in contrast, banish the word *estimate* from their vocabulary. When it comes to estimating, just say no!

"But you can never be exact," real estate investors have told me for years. "Close, maybe. But never exact."

I have a simple answer to that: *You have to be.* You simply can't afford to be inexact. You can't accept inexactness in yourself or in your real estate investment company.

You can't go to work every day believing that your company, the work you do, and the commitments you make are all too complex and unpredictable to be exact. With a mindset like that, you're doomed to run a sloppy ship. A ship that will eventually sink and suck you down with it.

This is so easy to avoid. Sloppiness—in both thought and action—is the root cause of your frustrations.

The solution to those frustrations is clarity. Clarity gives you the ability to set a clear direction, which fuels the momentum you need to grow your business.

Clarity, direction, momentum—they all come from insisting on exactness.

But how do you create exactness in a hopelessly inexact world? The answer is this. You discover the exactness in your company by refusing to do any work that can't be controlled exactly.

The only other option is to analyze the market, determine where the opportunities are, and then organize your company to be the exact provider of the services you've chosen to offer.

Two choices, and only two choices: (1) evaluate your company and then limit yourself to the tasks you know you can do exactly, or (2) start all over by analyzing the market, identifying the key opportunities in that market, and building a company that operates exactly.

What you cannot do, what you must refuse to do, from this day forward, is to allow yourself to operate with an inexact mindset. It will lead you to ruin.

Which leads us inexorably back to the word I have been using through this book: *systems.*

Who makes estimates? Only real estate investors who are unclear about exactly how to do the task in question. Only real estate investors whose experience has taught them that if something can go wrong, it will—and to them!

I'm not suggesting that a *systems solution* will guarantee that you always perform exactly as promised. But I am saying that a systems solution will faithfully alert you when you're going off track, and will do it before you have to pay the price for it.

In short, with a systems solution in place, your need to estimate will be a thing of the past, both because you have organized your company to anticipate mistakes, and because you have put into place the system to do something about those mistakes before they blow up.

There's this, too: To make a promise you intend to keep places a burden on you and your managers to dig deeply into how you intend to keep it. Such a burden will transform your intentions and increase your attention to detail.

With the promise will come dedication. With dedication will come integrity. With integrity will come consistency. With consistency will come results you can count on. And results you can count on mean that you get exactly what you hoped for at the outset of your company: the true pride of ownership that every real estate investor should experience.

This brings us to the subject of *clients*. Who are they? Why do they come to you? How can you identify yours? And who *should* your clients be? But first, let's find out what Than and Paul have to say about evaluating deals. ❧

www.michaelegerber.com/co-author

CHAPTER 14

Evaluating
Real Estate Deals

Than Merrill
Paul Esajian

Capital can do nothing without brains to direct it.

—J. Ogden Armour

In real estate, we make money when we buy—meaning that the equity is contained in the deal itself—and we realize that profit when we sell. So it is critical to implement a system that allows you to find a lot of high-margin deals, make a lot of offers, and shake out the rest of the junk.

In all seriousness, your income is directly related to the number of strategic offers you make each month. From the very beginning while launching your business, it is essential to implement an efficient system for filtering deals. In this chapter, we reveal our three-stage system that gives you a quick, structured way of finding deals that will bring consistent profits.

Depending on the marketing campaign you utilize, it will generally take ten to twenty-five leads to land one profitable deal. That's because most sellers are not "motivated" enough and want to sell their homes for retail market value or higher. As mentioned before, retail deals are houses priced at market rates, purchased by people who want to live in them or uneducated real estate investors who don't understand deals.

As professional investors, we seek deals that are available significantly below market value typically at 70 cents on the dollar or less. If we are buying rental properties, we also want to buy the property under market value, but we look more at the potential cash flow potential of the property.

You might think it's impossible to find deals at those kinds of prices. If you don't know how to market and lack systems to evaluate those leads, you probably will think they're impossible to come by. However, once you learn how to target motivated sellers and put the right systems in place, finding deals becomes a quick and easy process.

Let's dive into how our three-stage Deal Evaluation System works.

Stage I: Lead Intake

We get leads on properties from many different sources, but the majority of those leads come from the MLS, direct response marketing campaigns like direct mail, or referrals from other investors and real estate professionals. Using the MLS, we work with real estate agents to gather information about the property to evaluate the deal before going to see the house and possibly make an offer. With direct response marketing campaigns and referrals, we typically talk directly to the seller.

Let's start with the process when sellers contact our office directly. When a seller calls us, we need to build rapport and gather all the essential information about the property, the seller's situation, and the underlying financing. We enter this information into our database so that we can track the property as it moves through our pipeline. We use a seller-intake lead sheet to make sure we ask the same questions every time, and the whole process takes about ten minutes.

During the seller-intake process, we ask the seller many questions that ultimately lead us to judge whether it is a good deal. When asking questions, we want to find out the property's specifics, such as location, size, number of bedrooms and bathrooms, special features, and so forth. This enables us to run comparables to determine its value accurately. More importantly, we want to know the seller's motivation for selling and what sort of time frame he or she is looking to sell.

Highly motivated sellers include people going through a divorce, moving to another city, buying another house, or going through foreclosure. This tells us a lot about the potential of the deal, because if the seller is motivated to sell quickly, there is a good probability we can buy the property at a discount. Of course, we also want a property with equity, so that there's margin in the deal.

During the initial phone call, we also want to find out what the seller owes on the property and the terms of the underlying loan. This tells us two things. First, the information helps us to determine if there is any equity in the property. If the amount owed is less than the market value of the house, it has equity. Secondly, the loan balance helps us determine how we might structure our offer. If there is no mortgage or there is a very small mortgage, and the seller is motivated, we might make an offer asking for seller financing.

If the seller has equity but a high mortgage balance, it might be a good opportunity to buy the property "subject to" the existing mortgage. When you purchase a property subject to the existing financing, you leave the existing financing in place when you take title to the property—meaning the loan remains in the seller's name, title transfers to you as the buyer. It is important to note this is not the same as assuming the mortgage, when the loan is transferred to the buyer's name. We are not going to change the name of the borrower or sign for the debt when we buy a property subject to the existing mortgage.

On the phone, we also want to get an idea of the overall condition of the property and the type of repairs that might be needed. It will help us determine the current market value and the repair costs.

This will contrast with the after-repair value of the property—what the property will be worth once it is fixed up and sold at retail price.

Finally, we want to know all the details about the listing history—who owns the property and who is involved in the decision-making process. While we are speaking with the seller, we check out the seller's property by entering the address on zillow.com. The free website gives sales comparables on similar sold properties. It also gives a "zestimate," which is Zillow's estimate of the market value. The zestimate isn't highly accurate, but it gives you a ballpark idea of the property's value based on data aggregated from properties sold in the seller's area.

Zillow helps us judge if there's any equity or upside to this deal by comparing the property's zestimate with the seller's asking price. Essentially, we try to discern if the seller is looking for retail or willing to sell at a discounted price.

For example, Zillow might estimate that the house is worth $250,000. If the owner is seeking $250,000 to $350,000, he or she most likely is not a motivated seller. That gives us an idea of how much time to spend with the seller (not much!) and how to handle the lead. But if the seller is asking for a price that is far below Zillow's estimate, then we schedule an appointment right away to go see the property.

You should know your market area well enough so that when a seller calls you about a property, you have a fair idea of the price of properties in that area. Your intimate market knowledge will give you an advantage, because you can act with a sense of urgency when you come across a really good deal.

If someone does call you with a hot lead, do not let the seller think or shop your offer around. Get out to the property right away, analyze the deal, and make an offer. You might say, "What works better for you, Mr. Seller? 3:00 p.m. or 4:00 p.m.? Because I am going to be in the area around that time." (Heck, yeah, you're going to be in the area—you're going to be buying that property, remember?)

In this first stage, the amount of time spent on the phone is based on what the seller tells us. If the deal starts to look good, we spend a little more time building rapport with the seller. You also should have a really good elevator pitch about your business and what your business is all about, to give the seller confidence that you can help them with their situation and close the deal.

Here's how the opening conversation usually goes.

Than: "Thank you for calling CT Homes. This is Than Merrill. How can I help you?"

Seller: "I got your direct mail piece about how you guys buy properties. How exactly does this work?"

Than: "Great, thanks for calling. It's a really simple process. First, what's your name?"

Seller: "John."

Than: "Great, John. Well, we are a real estate investment company here in the San Diego area, and we buy a lot of homes in the area, in all conditions, from people just like you. You don't have to pay any commissions, and we can close on your timeline. The process is very easy. We gather some really basic information over the phone from you, and if it sounds like something we might be interested in, we will generally have an offer for you within 48 hours. So tell me, John, where is your property located?"

You don't need to memorize this sample conversation, because it won't seem natural when you're talking on the phone. The important thing is to hit the major benefit points that will pique the seller's interest and let him or her know that the process is very simple.

Depending on how you generate your leads, you might not always be talking to the sellers themselves. For example, we buy a lot of pre-foreclosures, REOs (real estate owned properties), and other distressed properties right off the MLS. When we pursue these types of properties, we speak directly with the listing agents. We evaluate these kinds of deals based on factors—such as the condition of the property, the potential after repair value of the property, and the willingness of the agent and seller to work with an investor.

No matter how the lead comes in or who we talk to, at this stage we are only gathering information and making some simple judgments about the deal's potential. We enter the lead and property information into our database to track the property through the process. We then move to the next stage.

Stage II: Desktop Evaluation

All leads on properties make it to this stage, but the majority of them will not make it to the next stage, because this is the point when we run sales comparables using the MLS. The MLS helps us determine the current "as is" market value of the property, as well as its after-repair value.

We classify the leads in our CRM system as we move them through the deal evaluation pipeline. In Stage II, we run comparables using both an MLS site and one or two non-MLS websites, such as zillow.com and trulia.com. The MLS sales comparables provide us much greater detail about the properties than the ones we get from Zillow or Trulia, so MLS makes our evaluation easier and more accurate.

The MLS has more accurate information because agents are required to input very detailed information about the properties they list. The MLS also has more photos of the comparable properties in the neighborhood than the other free websites.

How we run our comparables is very important as well. We always check comparables on properties that are within a half-mile radius of the property; within 20 percent of the square footage of the subject property; have the same number of bedrooms; and ideally have sold in the past six months.

Running comparables is the litmus test to figure out if the deal has potential. We then classify and rate the lead: it's either a *hot lead, a warm lead, a dead lead,* or an *agent referral lead.*

On *hot leads,* which have plenty of equity, we call back and schedule appointments to see the properties. If the seller is behind on payments and there is no equity, then we know we will have to negotiate a short sale with the bank. A short sale is when the mortgage amount is higher than the home's market value, and the bank is willing to accept less that what is owed as payment in full. With these types of sellers, we spend about 15 minutes on the phone explaining the short sale process and all the documents the seller will have to put together for us to be able to negotiate a short sale with a bank. These are hot leads, because the bank discounts can be significant, giving us high profits later.

On *warm leads*, we don't make an appointment; instead we call the seller or agent and make a verbal offer. If they don't think our verbal offer is in the zone of possible agreement, then we reclassify the lead as an *agent referral lead* (if the property is not already listed) or a *dead lead* if it is already listed in the MLS.

A lot of deals never make it to Stage III. When we evaluate twenty properties, we might schedule appointments to look at three or four of them after running comparables. Along the way, we track all this information, saving all the comparables, and making notes in our CRM database.

The CRM system is very powerful and allows us to automate our business. Many of our students use our CRM system to grow and scale their businesses. In fact, many have gone from just a few deals annually to multiple deals a month by utilizing our CRM technology.

Stage III: On-Site Property Evaluation

In the third stage, you will create what we call a comparable package of similar properties that have sold in the area that you can review before you visit the seller's property and make an offer. Our "repair estimate sheet" is in the comparable package; we use it when we are on-site to estimate repairs.

We take that information and put it in our buying appointment folder, which contains all the contracts and paperwork we will use to actually put the property under contract, if the seller accepts our offer. That folder also contains disclosures, a purchase and sale agreement, authorization to release agreement, and other essential documents. If the property is a short sale, we bring additional disclosures and short sale-specific documents.

At this point, we confirm the appointment over the phone and head out to look at the property and the other comparable properties. Typically, we want to look at three to five closed sales comparables (houses that sold) and two to three active comparables (houses currently listed for sale). If there are any comparables on deposit (in escrow and pending sale) in the immediate area, we look at those as well.

If you are dealing with out-of-state properties, you will need somebody to go look at them. This could be a person working with or for you or a real estate agent who can be trusted to make a proper evaluation.

If the property is in your area, you will look at it yourself or have a staff member do it. Once your business starts growing, you're going to have someone who just does acquisitions and manages this entire process on a daily basis.

Before heading out of the door, we make a financial evaluation using our "deal analyzer" software so we can determine exactly what we are going to offer for the property before we meet the seller or speak to the agent over the phone. The software we use to do this can be found at www.reiToolDemo.com.

Later, we can adjust our offer up or down, based on what repairs are needed inside the property. If the property looks like a fixer on the outside and needs a lot of work, generally it's going to be in the same condition inside. After we estimate the internal repairs, we close the deal with the seller or the agent and submit our written offer.

Wrapping It Up

The Deal Evaluation System requires organization, education, and training, but once it's in place, it gives us predictable and profit-
ults. This is why we are able to review hundreds of properties
h and narrow them down to the handful that we actually buy

each month. We use this system to run our multimillion-dollar real estate business.

Now let's see what revelations Michael has in store for us as he discusses the subject of clients. ✤

For more information about how we can help you as a real estate investor go to: www.MasteryForInvestors.com.

CHAPTER

15

On the Subject
of Clients

Michael E. Gerber

I don't build in order to have clients. I have clients in order to build.

—Ayn Rand

When it comes to the business of real estate investing, the best definition of clients I've ever heard is this:

Clients: *very special people who drive most real estate investors crazy.*

Does that work for you?

After all, it's a rare client who shows any appreciation for what a real estate investor has to go through to do the job as promised. Don't they always think the price is too high? And don't they focus on problems, broken promises, and the mistakes they think you make, rather than all the ways you bend over backward to give them what they need?

Do you ever hear other real estate investors voice these complaints? More to the point, have you ever voiced them yourself?

Well, you're not alone. I have yet to meet a real estate investor who doesn't suffer from a strong case of client confusion.

Client confusion is about:

- what your client really wants;
- how to communicate effectively with your client;
- how to keep your client happy;
- how to deal with client dissatisfaction; and
- whom to call a client.

Confusion 1: What Your Client Really Wants

Your clients aren't just people; they're very specific kinds of people. Let me share with you the six categories of clients as seen from the E-Myth marketing perspective: (1) tactile clients, (2) neutral clients, (3) withdrawal clients, (4) experimental clients, (5) transitional clients, and (6) traditional clients.

Your entire marketing strategy must be based on which type of client you are dealing with. Each of the six client types spends money on real estate investment services for very different, and identifiable, reasons. These are:

- Tactile clients get their major gratification from interacting with other people.
- Neutral clients get their major gratification from interacting with inanimate objects (computers, cars, information).
- Withdrawal clients get their major gratification from interacting with ideas (thoughts, concepts, stories).
- Experimental clients rationalize their buying decisions by perceiving that what they bought is new, revolutionary, and innovative.
- Transitional clients rationalize their buying decisions by perceiving that what they bought is dependable and reliable.
- Traditional clients rationalize their buying decisions by perceiving that what they bought is cost-effective, a good deal, and worth the money.

In short:

- If your client is tactile, you have to emphasize the *people* of your business.
- If your client is neutral, you have to emphasize the *technology* of your business.
- If your client is a withdrawal client, you have to emphasize the *idea* of your business.
- If your client is experimental, you have to emphasize the *uniqueness* of your business.
- If your client is transitional, you have to emphasize the *dependability* of your business.
- If your client is traditional, you have to talk about the *financial competitiveness* of your business.

What your clients want is determined by who they are. Who they are is regularly demonstrated by what they do. Think about the clients with whom you do business. Ask yourself: In which of the categories would I place them? What do they do for a living?

If your client is a mechanical engineer, for example, it's probably safe to assume he's a neutral client. If another one of your clients is a cardiologist, she's probably tactile. Accountants tend to be traditional, and software engineers are often experimental.

Having an idea about which categories your clients may fall into is very helpful to figuring out what they want. Of course, there's no exact science to it, and human beings constantly defy stereotypes. So don't take my word for it. You'll want to make your own analysis of the clients you serve.

Confusion 2: How to Communicate Effectively with Your Client

The next step in the client satisfaction process is to decide how to magnify the characteristics of your company that are most likely to appeal to your preferred category of client. That begins with what marketing people call your *positioning strategy*.

What do I mean by *positioning* your company? You position your company with words. A few well-chosen words to tell your clients exactly what they want to hear. In marketing lingo, those words are called your USP, or unique selling proposition.

For example, if you are targeting tactile clients (ones who love people), your USP could be: "Value Investing, where the feelings of people *really* count!"

If you are targeting experimental clients (ones who love new, revolutionary things), your USP could be: "Value Investing, where living on the edge is a way of life!" In other words, when they choose to schedule an appointment with you, they can count on both your services and equipment to be on the cutting edge of the real estate investment industry.

Is this starting to make sense? Do you see how the ordinary things most real estate investors do to get clients can be done in a significantly more effective way?

Once you understand the essential principles of marketing the E-Myth way, the strategies by which you attract clients can make an enormous difference in your market share.

Confusion 3: How to Keep Your Client Happy

Let's say you've overcome the first two confusions. Great. Now how do you keep your client happy?

Very simple . . . just keep your promise! And make sure your client *knows* you kept your promise every step of the way.

In short, giving your clients what they think they want is the key to keeping your clients (or anyone else, for that matter) really happy.

If your clients need to interact with people (high touch, tactile), make certain that they do.

If they need to interact with things (high-tech, neutral), make certain that they do.

If they need to interact with ideas (in their head, withdrawal), make certain that they do.

And so forth.

At E-Myth, we call this your *client fulfillment system*. It's the step-by-step process by which you do the task you've contracted to do and deliver what you've promised—on time, every time.

But what happens when your clients are *not* happy? What happens when you've done everything I've mentioned here and your client is still dissatisfied?

Confusion 4: How to Deal with Client Dissatisfaction

If you have followed each step up to this point, client dissatisfaction will be rare. But it can and will still occur—people are people, and some people will always find a way to be dissatisfied with something. Here's what to do about it:

- Always listen to what your clients are saying. And never interrupt while they're saying it.

- After you're sure you've heard all of your client's complaint, make absolutely certain you understand what she said by phrasing a question, such as: "Can I repeat what you've just told me, Ms. Harton, to make absolutely certain I understand you?"

- Secure your client's acknowledgment that you have heard her complaint accurately.

- Apologize for whatever your client thinks you did that dissatisfied her, even if you didn't do it!

- After your client has acknowledged your apology, ask her exactly what would make her happy.

- Repeat what your client told you would make her happy, and get her acknowledgment that you have heard correctly.

- If at all possible, give your client exactly what she has asked for.

You may be thinking, "But what if my client wants something totally impossible?" Don't worry. If you've followed my recommendations to the letter, what your client asks for will seldom seem unreasonable.

Confusion 5: Whom to Call a Client

At this stage, it's important to ask yourself some questions about the kind of clients you hope to attract to your company:

- Which types of clients would you most like to do business with?
- Where do you see your real market opportunities?
- Who would you like to work with, provide services to, and position your business for?

In short, *it's all up to you*. No mystery. No magic. Just a systematic process for shaping your company's future. But you must have the passion to pursue the process. And you must be absolutely clear about every aspect of it.

Until you know your clients as well as you know yourself.

Until all your complaints about clients are a thing of the past.

Until you accept the undeniable fact that client acquisition and client satisfaction are more science than art.

But unless you're willing to grow your company, you'd better not follow any of these recommendations. Because if you do what I'm suggesting, it's going to grow.

This brings us to the subject of *growth*. But first, let's see what Than and Paul have to say about marketing. ✤

www.michaelegerber.com/co-author

CHAPTER

16

Marketing to Get Great Deals

Than Merrill
Paul Esajian

The aim of marketing is to know and understand the customer so well the product or service fits him and sells itself.

—Peter F. Drucker

I n the late 1970s, two major companies were battling to dominate the video market. Sony's Betamax video standard was introduced in 1975, followed a year later by JVC's VHS. For the next few years the companies fought for market share. VHS eventually emerged as the winner while bitter Betamax owners cringed in their ever-decreasing corner of local video stores.

What makes this story unique is that the victory was not a result of VHS being a better product. In fact, Sony's Betamax was superior in many ways from a product standpoint. The war was won because JVC was better than Sony at marketing its product.

The lesson here is if you want market share or more deals than other investors in your local area, then what matters most is how you market. Marketing is the engine that drives your real estate business. Most aspects of your business will depend on successful marketing. Your overall marketing plan will entail foundational brand building, specific direct response campaigns, public relations, and business and self-promotion. Without effective marketing, your real estate business may offer the best service in your area, but no potential sellers or buyers will know about it.

When we work with new students we spend the majority of the first three months just ensuring they have the proper marketing strategies in place, so that the business can get off the ground successfully.

A real estate investor who doesn't know how to grow or structure a real estate business, but knows how to market, may not be operating optimally but still is missing the potential to make good money because they will have a lot of opportunities. However, if you know how to grow a business by implementing systems and you know how to market then you have a business set up for long-term sustainable success. You also have a business that has potential value if you were ever to decide you wanted to sell the business. A business is not only an entity for making profits but also something that you can market and sell in the future, as we've discussed. And that option should be everyone's end-all goal as it will lead you to developing this business the right way.

Marketing can be broken down into two major categories. First, you need foundational marketing materials to create a presence for your business in your area. Then you need strategic, direct response marketing campaigns to attract the types of leads that you seek.

Foundational Marketing

There are eight essential marketing tools every real estate investor must have when opening up shop: business cards, seller credibility packets, buyer credibility packets, a core website, an easy-to-remember phone number, a memorable business name, and a logo. These tools are used when you are meeting with sellers, buyers, lenders, and other real estate professionals. These resources will establish the identity and credibility of your business and be the foundation from which you build your brand. Once you have these basic marketing materials in place, you can start executing specific direct response marketing campaigns, which will generate the majority of your deals. Let's take a closer look at the items in your marketing arsenal.

Business Cards

A business card is an essential tool that all real estate investors must have. Throughout the course of your day, you often meet many people who want to know what line of business you're in. So the first step is to get a clean-looking business card.

Business cards will let people know you are in business, what you do, and can highlight the services you provide as an investor. They can also help to enhance your personal image. Production and printing costs are extremely low, but the benefits are immense.

We do recommend that you put a picture on your business card because studies have shown that people are more likely to hold on to a business card that has a photo on it. You want to differentiate yourself from others.

Seller Credibility Packet

When you meet with a seller, it is essential to build trust and rapport. Many times the sellers have no idea about you, but they responded to one of your marketing campaigns. That's why when you meet them for the first time it is essential to carry a packet of information to help establish your credibility. This packet is also what you can leave with the sellers after you make an offer on their property.

In fact, many sellers will reject your initial offer or need more time to think about it. So it is essential to provide information about your company that will continue to build trust after you leave. You want sellers to have additional information that they can flip through while they take a few days to mull over your offer. It will also help set you apart from other investors and real estate agents they may be meeting.

Your seller credibility packet should include your:

- full contact information (phone number, e-mail, website, and office address);
- core services your business offers sellers who don't necessarily want to sell through a real estate agent;
- any additional services your business provides that a seller would be interested in besides just selling their property. These could include relocation services, moving services, credit repair, and anything else that might benefit the seller;
- a description of your business and some basic personal information. Keep this brief. Most people don't care about you or your personal history. They want to know how you can help them and what's in it for them;
- testimonials from past sellers whose properties you have bought describing how easy it was to work with you and how professional you were. If you are brand new in the business, then put some testimonials together from any other real estate professionals you have dealt with or your accountant, attorney, insurance professional, or even an ex-girlfriend;
- a picture of you with a dog, a white jumpsuit, and one of those big, old, 1990s cell phones. We have seen a lot of real estate agents do this. It works. Do it. We dare you.

In all seriousness, whatever you do, make sure the packets are professionally printed and have some great, stock imagery that makes them look really nice. Lastly, make sure you always have some of these packets in your car at all times—you never know who you might bump into.

Buyer Credibility Packet

On the flip side, you will also be meeting with a lot of potential buyers when you are marketing your properties to sell. This is why it is also essential to have a buyer credibility packet.

Like a seller credibility packet, it should include your essential contact information, core services, additional services, business/personal information, and testimonials. The difference is everything—especially your services—should be geared towards buyers instead of sellers.

Private Money Credibility Packet

Obviously, raising money for your deals is an essential part of the business and this is why you must have a third packet of information. This credibility packet is geared toward private lenders who may be interested in funding your real estate deals. During the course of your daily interactions, you will meet many people who could be potential private lenders for your deals, and that's why you must have marketing materials that show people the opportunity to potentially earn a high rate of return as a lender.

A private money credibility packet is something you will give to a potential lender after you have established a relationship with them.

This packet should include your full contact information, company history, how private lending works, case studies of deals you have completed, your buying philosophy, the terms you offer, and testimonials from other lenders you have worked with. It should also include a very detailed section with answers to at least twenty of the most frequently asked questions that potential lenders have.

Core Website

Every successful real estate business has a dominant online presence. In fact, the majority of all sellers and buyers who are looking to sell or buy a property start the process by searching for solutions on the Internet.

You need to have a core website for your business that is professional looking and something you can use to establish credibility, generate leads, and sell/rent your properties.

We believe so strongly in this that we have created template websites that can be modified for all our coaching students. They can have a Web presence set up within twenty-four hours.

On your core website you should have the following:

- Home Page tab: This tab should include an overview of your company and what you do. On the upper right-hand corner of your website, you must have a place where a potential visitor can join your e-mail list. Your website is how you build your list of clients, and this is the most valuable asset of your business. On your home page you should also have full contact information so people can get a hold of you via phone or e-mail.

- About Us tab: This is a Web page where a visitor can get more detailed information about you, your company, and anybody who works for you.

- Sellers tab: When someone clicks on this tab, it sends the visitor to a page that speaks directly to sellers and discusses all the ways you can help them by purchasing their property. On this page you should have a Web form where sellers can begin the process by giving you some basic information about the property for sale so you can follow up with them.

- Buyers tab: This page on your site is geared specifically to buyers who are looking to purchase properties. You should have all your properties for sale on this page, as well as a Web form where potential buyers can submit their information so you can follow up with them.

- Blog tab: To keep content on your site fresh and to add value to your clients' lives, you should write one article a week that can be posted to your blog. This will help generate leads and is a great way to stay in touch and inform your clients. You could also rant and rave about politics and religion, if you want, but that would alienate half your clients.

- Properties for Rent tab: If you have a lot of rental inventory, this is where you can list your properties for rent.
- Resources tab: If you have great affiliate relationships with real estate-related products and services, you can list them here. You can also use this page to generate some affiliate income, which can help you expand your business.

Obviously, there are many other aspects of your website you can build out depending on the niche of real estate you are in, but I just want to outline the essentials.

Easy-to-Remember Phone Number

This is a ninja tip if you want to really enhance your marketing response rates. Get an easy-to-remember phone number, like cab companies do, that you can use in all your marketing campaigns. Your outdoor marketing response rates will be dramatically better when you have a number with repeating digits.

To get an easy-to-remember phone number, call your telephone service provider and ask what numbers are available with repeating digits. If you don't like the list of available numbers, then pick up the phone and start calling easy-to-remember numbers and start making offers. You will definitely find someone who is willing to sell their number for a couple hundred bucks. We have had numerous coaching students find great phone numbers this way.

Memorable Business Name

You need a memorable company name and an equally memorable Web URL that corresponds to your company name and conveys

what your business does. For example, a name like William Capital
Partners doesn't convey what the business does. However, Atlanta
Property Buyers would be a business name that would be more strategic, depending on the niche of the business you pursue. The bottom
line is that your business name should be strategically chosen and mean
something to a potential customer who is hearing it for the first time.

Logo and Business Color Schemes

Having a memorable logo and consistent color scheme will help
boost your response rates. There are a number of online services that can
create a relatively inexpensive logo. Your logo colors should ideally match
the look and feel of the colors you use in all your marketing materials.
The important point is to be consistent with the colors you choose.

Strategic Direct Response Marketing

Your marketing foundation establishes the much-needed credibility for your business and will help you generate referral leads—people
sending leads to you. Once your marketing foundation is in place, you
will then want to begin executing strategic direct response marketing
campaigns. These are campaigns targeting potentially motivated sellers
and buyers. These campaigns will also be responsible for the majority of
the leads you get on a monthly basis.

A direct response marketing campaign is any marketing strategy
that is designed to elicit a direct response from a sub-section of people.
Generally, it compels the person to either pick up the phone and call or
fill out and submit a Web form online. In either circumstance, you are
able to capture their contact information when they take an action.

So let's discuss a few of the direct response campaigns we use in
our business.

Direct Mail

We have used direct mail to find some of our best deals over the years. Direct mail is highly effective when you target the right list, have a compelling message, and have consistency. You can do Google searches to find companies in your area with direct mail lists you can buy.

The best direct mail lists to target are:

- Pre-foreclosure lists: These are lists of homeowners who are behind on their payments and are in the process of being foreclosed upon by the lender.

- Probate lists: These are homeowners who have passed away and the ownership is in the process of being transferred from the deceased to their heirs.

- Bankruptcy lists: We target property owners who were recently dismissed from being in bankruptcy. More often than not the property owners used the bankruptcy process to stall the pending foreclosure.

- Free and Clear landlord lists: These are rental properties that are owned by landlords and there is no debt against the property. These properties obviously have a lot of equity so term deals can be negotiated.

Your direct mail message should be geared towards the list that you are targeting and should explain how you can buy the property directly from the recipient. It is very important to differentiate yourself from real estate agents who charge commissions and hope to find a buyer. Essentially, you are an alternative solution and you can pay cash, close quickly, and take the property in "as is" condition. You also can be extremely flexible on the closing date, since you won't be living in the property. These things should definitely be part of your marketing message.

Consistency is vitally important to the success of your direct mail campaign. We hit most of the lists we target with at least four different direct mail pieces. In fact, you are better off hitting a smaller section of the list four times than you are hitting the whole list one time.

Finally, you will want to use a direct mail fulfillment company to help you execute the mailings. Once we did this, we offloaded several hours of work each week; what used to take us ten to fifteen hours of work per week now takes us fifteen minutes.

Bandit Signs

Bandit signs are small signs made of corrugated plastic that have a very simple marketing message like "We Buy Houses Cash" with a phone number. In fact, you have probably seen these signs by other investors around town. They usually cost less than $2 a piece and can be placed in high-traffic areas. Please be aware that certain municipalities have sign ordinances that you must know and comply with.

Online Lead Capture Pages (Mini-Sites)

Online lead capture pages are highly optimized websites built around capturing traffic from high-quality search terms that motivated sellers and buyers type into the major search engines. The difference between these mini-sites and your core website is that these mini-sites are highly optimized for one specific keyword that has high search volume and low competition. The structure of these sites utilizes all the proper search engine optimization (SEO) techniques, so they show up for the one search term you are targeting.

On the website itself, you should have a video that gives the prospect a compelling reason to opt in via a Web form. That way, a lead is generated. The video itself should be designed to solve a problem the sellers or buyers may have based on the search term they are using.

When you build up a portfolio of these sites, they can literally generate hundreds of leads for you every single month, which can have a major positive impact on your business. We delve into more on this topic in Chapter 20.

How Many Campaigns Should You Implement?

When you're starting your business, you should execute three to five strategic direct response marketing campaigns every month. The reason you want multiple campaigns going out at once is because you never want your business to be dependent on just one source of leads. If that one source were to dry up, it could be very costly for your business as you tested and implemented other campaigns.

It is also important to note that most real estate rookies give up on their marketing campaigns way too early. Marketing is a process of testing and tweaking until you get the desired response rates you need to make the campaign pay off.

That is why so many people leverage the systems we have already created in our real estate investing business. Many of our coaching students use our marketing campaigns and marketing plan. They understand the value of consistent leads and don't want to gamble on campaigns they are not sure are going to work or bring a return on their investment.

Wrapping It Up

Once you have a marketing campaign that works, you want to scale and automate it as quickly as possible. Marketing consistency requires an automated fulfillment system that you can easily tap month after month. It's an important cornerstone of your business that you want to have in place, so that it can constantly generate new leads and thus new profits down the line. Remember, it isn't the most knowledgeable investor who gets the deal. It's the investor who has the most consistent marketing systems.

Now let's consider Michael's thoughts about growth. ♣

For more information about how we can help you as a real estate investor go to: www.MasteryForInvestors.com.

17

On the Subject of Growth

Michael E. Gerber

Growth is the only evidence of life.
    —John Henry Newman, *Apologia Pro Vita Sua*

The rule of business growth says that every business, like every child, is destined to grow. Needs to grow. Is determined to grow.

Once you've created your real estate investment company, once you've shaped the idea of it, the most natural thing for it to do is to . . . *grow!* And if you stop it from growing, it will die.

Once a real estate investor has started a company, it's his or her job to help it grow. To nurture it and support it in every way. To infuse it with

- Purpose
- Passion
- Will
- Belief

- Personality
- Method

As your company grows, it naturally changes. And as it changes from a small company to something much bigger, you will begin to feel out of control. News flash: that's because you *are* out of control.

Your company *has* exceeded your know-how, sprinted right past you, and now it's taunting you to keep up. That leaves you two choices: grow as big as your company demands you grow, or try to hold your company at its present level—at the level you feel most comfortable.

The sad fact is that most real estate investors do the latter. They try to keep their company small, securely within their comfort zone. Doing what they know how to do, what they feel most comfortable doing. It's called playing it safe.

But as the company grows, the number, scale, and complexity of tasks will grow, too, until they threaten to overwhelm the real estate investor. More people are needed. More space. More money. Everything seems to be happening at the same time. A hundred balls are in the air at once.

As I've said throughout this book: Most real estate investors are not entrepreneurs. They aren't true businesspeople at all, but technicians suffering from an entrepreneurial seizure. Their philosophy of coping with the workload can be summarized as "just do it," rather than figuring out how to get it done through other people using innovative systems to produce consistent results.

Given most real estate investors' inclination to be the master juggler in their company, it's not surprising that as complexity increases, as work expands beyond their ability to do it, as money becomes more elusive, they are just holding on, desperately juggling more and more balls. In the end, most collapse under the strain.

You can't expect your company to stand still. You can't expect your company to stay small. A company that stays small and depends on you to do everything isn't a company—it's a job!

Yes, just like your children, your business must be allowed to grow, to flourish, to change, to become more than it is. In this way, it will match your vision. And you know all about vision, right? You'd better. It's what you do best!

Do you feel the excitement? You should. After all, you know what your company *is* but not what it *can be*.

It's either going to grow or die. The choice is yours, but it is a choice that must be made. If you sit back and wait for change to overtake you, you will always have to answer no to this question: Are you ready?

This brings us to the subject of *change*. But first, let's see what Than and Paul have to say about growth. ✤

www.michaelegerber.com/co-author

18

How to Grow Intelligently

Than Merrill
Paul Esajian

When a bonsai stops growing, you know it's dead.

—Japanese Proverb

Real estate investors are vital drivers of today's economy, so it is imperative you do all you can to ensure your business doesn't just survive, but thrive to compete in today's market. In order to thrive, you will need to grow the number and frequency of flips, so that you reach the volume of deals needed for a sustainable and scaleable business.

The challenge is that real estate investing is not completely scalable, because every property and every situation you encounter will be unique. So you must utilize what we call "smart growth patterns." You need to understand your capacity to grow, and make sure you grow fast but only at the rate at which you can improve systems, implement technology, and recruit talent.

159

Smart Ways to Grow

You have to know your boundaries. Some of the most dangerous real estate investors are not the brand-new ones who have never done a deal; they are the relatively new investors who have completed a few successful transactions and begin to overestimate their abilities to handle multiple deals simultaneously.

Brand-new investors are usually so conservative, risk-averse, and fearful that they bypass many deals that don't have enough profit or aren't absolutely the right ones, so then their first project is profitable.

However, after completing a few deals, these investors can become overconfident, causing them to acquire marginal deals or take on too many projects at once. Often, they may be under-capitalized or their business, staff, processes, or technology may not be able to handle more than one deal at a time. These investors risk having the whole house of cards come tumbling down on top of themselves.

This is why it is so important to never let your ego get ahead of your business and why you must never stop learning. When investors start to believe they know it all, something bad usually happens or the market turns and their lack of education hurts them.

A real estate business should have a very steady pattern of growth when you focus on one or two property types. When you stay focused on a particular type of property, it becomes easier to scale and grow than when you jump from lease options to rehabs, from shopping centers to office building. When you start building your business, you need to stick to one or maybe two sectors, and master those sectors before you move to another one.

Improving Business Processes

Let's take a look at how you can improve business processes. A lot of times you don't need enhanced technology initially or more staff in order to grow. You just need to have more efficient processes and spend less time on each transaction. In order to accomplish this goal, you should map out and document each process that you are trying to improve.

Let us give you a practical example of a process that produces amazing results in building systems around almost every area of our business. One of the tools we absolutely love to use for brainstorming ideas, organizing projects, and creating systems is a mind-mapping software called MindManager, available at www.mindjet.com. There are many other software programs, but we found this to be the most user-friendly and productive. Whenever we identify an activity that repeats more than a couple of times in our business, we start documenting the steps on a mind map. The goal is to create a reminder checklist and a predictable outcome from start to finish.

One such activity is the closing process when buying a property. For each property, we put all the steps involved in closing a transaction on the mind map, and then we get feedback from team members involved in the transaction to fill in anything we might have forgotten. The real test comes when we start using these maps as checklists to make sure we follow the same procedure while closing every deal. As we use these mind maps from transaction to transaction, they continue evolving with additional hints, reminders, and variations. Once this process is started, it becomes an organic system that literally builds on itself. We've repeated this process in nearly every area of our business.

Over the years, we've built hundreds of these systems, from marketing systems for direct mail to sales processes for selling homes to online systems for building awesome lead-generation campaigns online.

We create reporting documents to track the progress of anyone who works the system. For example, a document might track how many sales leads came in a month, how many of those leads we visited, how many offers were made, and how many closed. By tracking these numbers in reports, we can create monthly goals. By the time we hire someone to replace one of us as a *technician*, while the original employee steps into the new role of *manager*, the job is a systematized process with clear-cut goals. After we define the manager's role overseeing the system, we can then hire someone else to replace us as *manager.* This frees us from the department as a whole, so we can focus on the role of *entrepreneur.*

When you do this in all areas of your real estate business, you can work on driving revenue, opening new locations, or launching another business.

Improving Technology

When we do technology audits on coaching students' businesses, we're shocked to see the antiquated technology systems they use to process their deals and run their business. The tools they choose range from Microsoft Outlook to yellow legal pads, from sticky notes to rudimentary paper filing systems. As a result, a good portion of their time is spent looking for the 123 Main Street file they have buried beneath a stack of papers.

Obviously, it is very difficult to grow and scale if you are running your business like that.

Take a look at Geico, for example, if you want to see a huge company that has superior business processes. When you call Geico to get an insurance quote, your name goes into a CRM, a lead is created, information is gathered about your situation, and you are then moved through a sales pipeline until you buy insurance. Once you buy insurance, your interaction with that business is not over. You are then moved to a marketing campaign that will give you information about Geico's other products and services.

This business process leverages everything from websites to a CRM to a sales force working the leads. It is optimized to take the client from a lead to a sale, which is how revenue is generated.

Your real estate business should follow the same design process. This is why you have to make sure that everything from your website to your CRM to your marketing campaigns are all integrated into your daily business processes. Instead of selling insurance, you are selling houses. The product is different, but not the process.

Over the years we have used various technology platforms in order to streamline and automate activities within the business. At first, we patched together a lot of independent systems, but we often found this to be problematic, because all the information wasn't stored in one place. Likewise, we had employees who lacked certain technical skills and could only access certain programs, so sometimes the information we needed for each deal was scattered throughout the office.

To fix this problem, we all got together and decided that we needed to invest in a specific real estate platform that could combine all these systems.

Luckily, we found a great solution that integrated our Web presence, marketing platform, contact management, deal management, and employee management into one easy-to-use platform. After years of using the platform and loving it, we created a great relationship with the owner of the company. We ended up investing in the company and are now a minority owner. To see a demo of the software we use, visit www.reiToolDemo.com.

There simply is no substitute for having systems in place that provide critical information on things like marketing performance, property inventory, deal status updates, client conversation notes, and financial information. The key to a successful, growing business is a healthy obsession for and successful adoption of automation. Pay attention to every detail and do regular technology audits of your systems. Then whenever you feel it's necessary, adjust your system, as long as it doesn't shut down your business.

Improving People

Hiring the right people can help grow your business astronomically and make your life a heck of a lot easier as the head of your organization. At the same time you can create a culture where people enjoy being around and make the hours you spend working enjoyable. Having the right people can also help you grow personally as they will push you to become a better person personally and professionally.

People, like systems, need to be improved continually. This would include everyone from your direct employees to real estate associates who are involved in your transactions. We invest in our team members heavily because we realize that as they gain experience and knowledge, our business will also develop. We are constantly challenging our team members to grow by reading books and industry trade journals, attending seminars, and getting coaching. Most people have a natural desire to grow and will embrace a culture where an emphasis is placed on personal growth.

Improving Revenue Streams

To grow intelligently, you should always be raising money and looking to leverage more competencies and boost revenue streams within your core business. Here's a great example of how we did it with affiliated services, as mentioned before.

During our first full year of business, our only revenue streams came from flipping properties and buying and holding deals. One day we realized that numerous buyer and seller leads we generated each month could create additional revenue streams. Many of the sellers and buyers we worked with and were on our e-mail list would frequently ask us for referrals for other real estate-related services and products. We realized that people in our company had become a trusted source of information for our clients. We also discovered that we could get paid for the recommendations we did of companies and services.

For example, we had hundreds of sellers calling us each month looking for a viable solution in selling their property. As investors we would analyze the deal and make an offer, but for many of the sellers the price we offered was just too low. However, our interaction with the sellers was still positive, and because of that, many of them were open to our recommendations for a real estate agent in the area who could sell their home at the price they were looking for. After referring many leads to two real estate agents, we decided to take the listings in-house. Than got his license and hired another agent to work under him so that we could properly service the clients whose homes we listed.

As we said earlier, we strongly encourage investors to get a real estate agent's or broker's license, if they don't have one already. We have a very profitable brokerage business and a lot of the leads that feed it are generated from our investment business.

Over time, we found a list of great companies that had products and services our buyers and sellers needed, and we began to profit in other ways as well. For instance, a lot of our buyers needed credit repair in order to qualify to buy a home from us. So, we established a great relationship with a credit repair company that paid us an affiliate commission every time we referred a client.

These various affiliate relationships quickly ended up funding our entire monthly marketing budget; later they grew into a business by itself. Affiliate marketing income streams will expand your capital base, boost your bottom line, and set you up for future growth. This money goes straight to the bottom line because you have already spent your time, energy, or strategic marketing dollars to generate these leads. All you're doing now is creating another revenue source from leads that are just sitting in your database.

Preparing for Growth

If you want to grow, you have to know where you want to go. And to get there, your goal must be to transition from a business that is dependent on you to a business that is dependent on systems and other people.

We have covered a tremendous amount of ground so far on how to do this. However, we will ask you the same question we ask many of our students: What is stopping you from taking the action needed to reengineer your business and, therefore, your life?

If you believe you can build a successful business that is not dependent on you, then this will become your reality. If you tell us it won't work for your business or in your area, then there is a good chance this will become your reality. This type of defeatist thinking can seal your own fate and is what needs to change first, before anything else can.

Wrapping It Up

Growth is about being open to new ideas and realizing that you will never know it all and that every area of your business can improve. Smart growth is about working strategically on those areas of your business that need the most work. Smart growth is about staying focused on improving business processes, integrating technology, improving people, leveraging your client list, and finally fixing any "stinking thinking" that you might have.

Chances are if you have gotten this far, you are beginning to get a glimpse of what your business and life could be like. You are beginning to imagine how it will feel six or twelve months from now when your business is running optimally without your constant involvement. Hold on to that vision and let it drive you to where you want to go, because everything starts with the decision to make a change.

On that note, let's discover in the next chapter what Michael has to say about change. ✤

For more information about how we can help you as a real estate investor go to: www.MasteryForInvestors.com.

On the Subject of Change

Michael E. Gerber

There is nothing permanent except change.
—Heraclitus of Ephesus, *Lives of the Philosophers*

So your company is growing. That means, of course, that it's also changing. Which means it's driving you and everyone in your life crazy.

That's because, to most people, change is a diabolical thing. Tell most people they've got to change, and their first instinct is to crawl into a hole. Nothing threatens their existence more than change. Nothing cements their resistance more than change. Nothing.

Yet for the past thirty-five years, that's exactly what I've been proposing to small-business owners: the need to change. Not for the sake of change itself, but for the sake of their lives.

I've talked to countless real estate investors whose hopes weren't being realized through their company; whose lives were consumed by work; who slaved increasingly longer hours for decreasing pay; whose dissatisfaction grew as their enjoyment shriveled; whose company had become the worst job in the world; whose money was out of control; whose employees were a source of never-ending hassles, just like their clients, their bank, and, increasingly, even their families.

More and more, these real estate investors spent their time alone, dreading the unknown and anxious about the future. And even when they were with people, they didn't know how to relax. Their mind was always on the job. They were distracted by work, by the thought of work. By the fear of falling behind.

And yet, when confronted with their condition and offered an alternative, most of the same real estate investors strenuously resisted. They assumed that if there were a better way of doing business, they already would have figured it out. They derived comfort from knowing what they believed they already knew. They accepted the limitations of being a real estate investor; or the truth about people; or the limitations of what they could expect from their clients, their employees, their team members, their bankers—even their family and friends.

In short, most real estate investors I've met over the years would rather live with the frustrations they already have than risk enduring new frustrations.

Isn't that true of most people you know? Rather than opening up to the infinite number of possibilities life offers, they prefer to shut their life down to respectable limits. After all, isn't that the most reasonable way to live?

I think not. I think we must learn to let go. I think that if you fail to embrace change, it will inevitably destroy you.

Conversely, by opening yourself to change, you give your real estate investment company the opportunity to get the most from your talents.

Let me share with you an original way to think about change, about life, about who we are and what we do. About the stunning notion of expansion and contraction.

Contraction versus Expansion

"Our salvation," a wise man once said, "is to allow." That is, to be open, to let go of our beliefs, to change. Only then can we move from a point of view to a viewing point.

That wise man was Thaddeus Golas, the author of a small, powerful book entitled *The Lazy Man's Guide to Enlightenment* (Seed Center, 1971).

Among the many inspirational things he had to say was this compelling idea:

> *The basic function of each being is expanding and contracting. Expanded beings are permeative; contracted beings are dense and impermeative. Therefore each of us, alone or in combination, may appear as space, energy, or mass, depending on the ratio of expansion to contraction chosen, and what kind of vibrations each of us expresses by alternating expansion and contraction. Each being controls his own vibrations.*

In other words, Golas tells us that the entire mystery of life can be summed up in two words: *expansion* and *contraction*. He goes on to say:

> *We experience expansion as awareness, comprehension, understanding, or whatever we wish to call it.*
>
> *When we are completely expanded, we have a feeling of total awareness, of being one with all life.*
>
> *At that level we have no resistance to any vibrations or interactions of other beings. It is timeless bliss, with unlimited choice of consciousness, perception, and feeling.*
>
> *When a [human] being is totally contracted, he is a mass particle, completely imploded.*
>
> *To the degree that he is contracted, a being is unable to be in the same space with others, so contraction is felt as fear, pain, unconsciousness, ignorance, hatred, evil, and a whole host of strange feelings.*
>
> *At an extreme [of contraction, a human being] has the feeling of being completely insane, of resisting everyone and everything, of being unable to choose the content of his consciousness.*

Of course, these are just the feelings appropriate to mass vibra-
tion levels, and he can get out of them at any time by expanding,
by letting go of all resistance to what he thinks, sees, or feels.

Stay with me here. Because what Golas says is profoundly important. When you're feeling oppressed, overwhelmed, exhausted by
more than you can control—contracted, as Golas puts it—you can
change your state to one of expansion.

According to Golas, the more contracted we are, the more threatened by change; the more expanded we are, the more open to change.

In our most enlightened—that is, open—state, change is as
welcome as non-change. Everything is perceived as a part of ourselves.
There is no inside or outside. Everything is one thing. Our sense of
isolation is transformed to a feeling of ease, of light, of joyful relationship with everything.

As infants, we didn't even think of change in the same way,
because we lived those first days in an unthreatened state. Insensitive
to the threat of loss, most young children are only aware of *what is.*
Change is simply another form of *what is.* Change just *is.*

However, when we are in our most contracted—that is, closed—
state, change is the most extreme threat. If the known is what I have,
then the unknown must be what threatens to take away what I
have. Change, then, is the unknown. And the unknown is fear. It's
like being between trapezes.

- To the fearful, change is threatening because things may
  get worse.
- To the hopeful, change is encouraging because things may
  get better.
- To the confident, change is inspiring because the challenge
  exists to improve things.

If you are fearful, you see difficulties in every opportunity. If you
are fear-free, you see opportunities in every difficulty.

Fear protects what I have from being taken away. But it also
disconnects me from the rest of the world. In other words, fear keeps
me separate and alone.

Here's the exciting part of Golas's message: with this new understanding of contraction and expansion, we can become completely attuned to where we are at all times.

If I am afraid, suspicious, skeptical, and resistant, I am in a contracted state. If I am joyful, open, interested, and willing, I am in an expanded state. Just knowing this puts me on an expanded path. Always remembering this, Golas says, brings enlightenment, which opens me even more.

Such openness gives me the ability to freely access my options. And taking advantage of options is the best part of change. Just as there are infinite ways to greet a client, there are infinite ways to run your company. If you believe Thaddeus Golas, your most exciting option is to be open to all of them.

Because your life is lived on a continuum between the most contracted and most expanded—the most closed and most open—states, change is best understood as the movement from one to the other, and back again.

Most small-business owners I've met see change as a thing in itself, as something that just happens to them. Most experience change as a threat. Whenever change shows up at the door, they quickly slam it. Many bolt the door and pile up the furniture. Some even run for their gun.

Few of them understand that change isn't a thing in itself, but rather the manifestation of many things. You might call it the revelation of all possibilities. Think of it as the ability at any moment to sacrifice what we are for what we could become.

Change can either challenge us or threaten us. It's our choice. Our attitude toward change can either pave the way to success or throw up a roadblock.

Change is where opportunity lives. Without change we would stay exactly as we are. The universe would be frozen still. Time would end.

At any given moment, we are somewhere on th[e]
a contracted and expanded state. Most of us are in th[e]
journey, neither totally closed nor totally open. Acc[o]

172 The E-Myth Real Estate Investor

change is our movement from one place in the middle toward one of the two ends.

Do you want to move toward contraction or toward enlightenment? Because without change, you are hopelessly stuck with what you've got.

Without change,

- we have no hope;
- we cannot know true joy;
- we will not get better; and
- we will continue to focus exclusively on what we have and the threat of losing it.

All of this negativity contracts us even more, until, at the extreme closed end of the spectrum, we become a black hole so dense that no light can get in or out.

Sadly, the harder we try to hold on to what we've got, the less able we are to do so. So we try still harder, which eventually drags us even deeper into the black hole of contraction.

Are you like that? Do you know anybody who is?

Think of change as the movement between where we are and where we're not. That leaves only two directions for change: either moving forward or slipping backward. We become either more contracted or more expanded.

The next step is to link change to how we feel. If we feel afraid, change is dragging us backward. If we feel open, change is pushing us forward.

Change is not a thing in itself, but a movement of our consciousness. By tuning in, by paying attention, we get clues to the state of our being.

Change, then, is not an outcome or something to be acquired. Change is a shift of our consciousness, of our being, of our humanity, of our attention, of our relationship with all other beings in the universe.

We are either "more in relationship" or "less in relationship." Change is the movement in either of those directions. The exciting part is that *we possess the ability to decide which way we go . . . and to now, in the moment, which way we're moving.*

Closed, open . . . Open, closed. Two directions in the universe. The choice is yours.

Do you see the profound opportunity available to you? What an extraordinary way to live!

Enlightenment is not reserved for the sainted. Rather, it comes to us as we become more sensitive to ourselves. Eventually, we become our own guides, alerting ourselves to our state, moment by moment: *open . . . closed . . . open . . . closed.*

Listen to your inner voice, your ally, and feel what it's like to be open and closed. Experience the instant of choice in both directions.

You will feel the awareness growing. It may be only a flash at first, so be alert. This feeling is accessible, but only if you avoid the black hole of contraction.

Are you afraid that you're totally contracted? Don't be—it's doubtful. The fact that you're still reading this book suggests that you're moving in the opposite direction.

You're more like a running back seeking the open field. You can see the opportunity gleaming in the distance. In the open direction.

Understand that I'm not saying that change itself is a point on the path; rather, it's the all-important movement.

Change is *in you*, not *out there.*

What path are you on? The path of liberation? Or the path of crystallization?

As we know, change can be for the better or for the worse.

If change is happening *inside* of you, it is for the worse only if you remain closed to it. The key, then, is your attitude—your acceptance or rejection of change. Change can be for the better only if you accept it. And it will certainly be for the worse if you don't.

Remember, change is nothing in itself. Without you, change doesn't exist. Change is happening inside of each of us, giving us clues to where we are at any point in time.

Rejoice in change, for it's a sign you are alive.

Are we open? Are we closed? If we're open, good things are bound to happen. If we're closed, things will only get worse.

According to Golas, it's as simple as that. Whatever happens defines where we are. *How* we are is *where* we are. It cannot be any other way.

For change is life.

Charles Darwin wrote, "It is not the strongest of the species that survive, nor the most intelligent, but the one that proves itself most responsive to change."

The growth of your real estate investment company, then, is its change. Your role is to go with it, to be with it, to share the joy, embrace the opportunities, meet the challenges, learn the lessons.

Remember, there are three kinds of people: (1) those who make things happen, (2) those who let things happen, and (3) those who wonder what the hell happened. The people who make things happen are masters of change. The other two are its victims.

Which type are you?

The Big Change

If all this is going to mean anything to the life of your company, you have to know when you're going to leave it. At what point, in your company's rise from where it is now to where it can ultimately grow, are you going to sell it? Because if you don't have a clear picture of when you want out, your company is the master of your destiny, not the reverse.

As we stated earlier, the most valuable form of money is equity, and unless your business vision includes your equity and how you will use it to your advantage, you will forever be consumed by your company.

Your company is potentially the best friend you ever had. It is your company's nature to serve you, so let it. If, however, you are not a wise steward, if you do not tell your company what you expect from it, it will run rampant, abuse you, use you, and confuse you.

Change. Growth. Equity.

Focus on the point in the future when you will take leave of your company. Now reconsider your goals in that context. Be specific. Write them down.

Skipping this step is like tiptoeing through earthquake country. Who can say where the fault lies waiting? And who knows exactly when your whole world may come crashing down around you?

Which brings us to the subject of *time*. But first, let's see what Than and Paul have to say about change. ♣

www.michaelegerber.com/co-author

CHAPTER
20

The Next-Generation Real Estate Investor

Than Merrill
Paul Esajian

The best way to predict the future is to create it.

—Peter F. Drucker

As a real estate investor, you must learn how to adapt to change. The market will always be changing, along with every other aspect of the industry. We've been part of this industry for many years and we've seen all types of investors—especially those with a shortsighted, "if it ain't broke, don't fix it" attitude—come and go. The more quickly you can continually adapt to change as part of your growth strategy, the more likely you will succeed in this fast-paced, intensely competitive environment.

Fear can be our greatest motivator in embracing change. However, we choose to focus on another motivator—learning. This approach is rooted in the love for learning and the immense satisfaction you can get from the entrepreneurial creativity in running your own business. As an investor, whenever you are in an environment where you are constantly adapting, learning is a necessary and rewarding companion. This is what truly makes real estate investing stimulating and fulfilling, aside from the money it can generate.

But learning alone doesn't pay the bills or help you secure prosperity. This is why in all our trainings we put so much emphasis on practical implementation and systems for running a real estate investing business. Let us give you some insight into how we have embraced change in evolving markets by harnessing a competitive online strategy.

Constantly Evolving Markets

In the real estate investing world, change happens on multiple levels. First, the economic conditions, and therefore markets, are subject to constant pressures and changes. This means you have to adapt to new cycles and strategies in order to capitalize on new sources of opportunities.

We have a large network of students across the country, so we stay in tune with national market trends. We always help new students identify what the best niche and investment strategies are in their markets. When market conditions change, it's important to stay one step ahead of everyone else, so that you can protect your business and act on new opportunities before most investors are even aware of them.

The Zillow and Google Effects

The methods and tools of research, marketing, and reaching your clients to complete deals evolve constantly. This is mainly due to improvements in technology and the growing availability of information online. We like to call this phenomenon the Zillow Effect. Websites like Zillow.com and Trulia.com have sprung up all over the Internet and offer a vast amount of free real estate-related information to the public. This has made the market much more transparent to average sellers and buyers. It has also made it a lot easier for new investors to study the market. Both investors and property owners are able to know values and spot trends in local and national markets. All this presents opportunities as well as challenges for real estate investors.

Let's start with the positive effect this has had on the real estate business. Everything is online these days. Marketing and research activities used to require frustrating and time-consuming trips to the county or city clerk's office to search for ownership information or used to require exclusive access to services such as MLS. But they are now accessible to anyone with a computer and Internet connection. If you fear technology and don't know how to efficiently access, filter, and process this deluge of information, then you could lose your competitive advantage to someone who embraces technology.

Making sense of all this data is one of the biggest hurdles for new investors, who frequently are overwhelmed, which leads to analysis paralysis. As a real estate investor, you have to quickly cut through excess information, identify vital numbers, and make quick, yet calculated decisions. We stress: intelligent and calculated decisions. This business is not about gambling. As a matter of fact, we hate gambling. In business and in life, we put ourselves in the best position to win over and over again and stack the cards in our favor *every* time. By understanding how to leverage access to this information to your benefit, you can move quickly on opportunities and always be on to the very best and most-profitable deals without subjecting your business to unnecessary risk.

However, sellers and buyers are much more educated these days and also have access to much of the same market information as investors. This is why your level of knowledge, creative problem solving, and flexibility to make decisions and act quickly will allow you to make money as an investor. We want to make one point clear: we always take a "win win win" approach, where all parties walk away from a transaction satisfied, so it's not a matter of trying to misinform anyone in the process. It is, however, important that you can effectively educate customers on why they should work with your company and enlighten them about the factors that play into every real estate transaction. These factors can include solutions to personal situations, industry know-how, timeline, and other benefits of working with investors versus other available alternatives.

The Zillow Effect plays into factors related to availability of information, but another phenomenon has been forcing investors to embrace change. Nothing is changing faster than the online world and methods of marketing online. We call this the Google Effect. It is simply no longer sufficient to have a good story to tell buyers and sellers about why they should do business with you. Today's sellers and buyers expect higher sophistication from investors, and this frequently starts with an online presence that proves your credibility. Real estate investors who don't subscribe to treating investing as a business and to establishing credibility online lose out to those who do.

A Web presence is no longer a "nice to have" novelty; it is a vital part of doing business as a real estate investor. This means you must have a compelling business website. It means your business must have social media presence and lead capture websites (more on these below). If you expect your business to show up in strategic online searches then you must understand the basics of SEO (search engine optimization). We have a specific three-day training where we work with our coaching students on developing their Web presence. It's not something that you can learn by just searching the Internet or reading a book.

Likewise, as we discuss later in this chapter, you should have a CRM or some sort of database to manage all your deals and data on the properties you buy and sell.

Online Strategy

There are many components of creating an effective online presence. Understanding how the components interact is vital for your success. We could write a whole book on just this topic alone, but let us give you some insight into a few examples of what we teach and how we help set up our coaching students for success.

We start building their online strategy by identifying the most important activity in the business, which is marketing and lead generation. After all, if you don't have leads, you really don't have a business. And this is true not only for real estate investors, but for any business. Unfortunately, traditional websites and online strategies simply don't stack up in today's competitive environment.

Firstly, simply being found online can be challenging. You are competing with literally thousands of websites. Next, even if you are found, customers make instant judgments about your business based on your website, so make it your mission to create a good first impression, capture readers' attention, and provide immediate value. Lastly, "old school" methods of putting up a brochure site don't produce results, because even if you manage to drive enough traffic to the site and capture the attention of your prospects, it doesn't mean they will be ready to do business with you at that particular moment.

Converting website visitors to happy customers is therefore all about the combined process of building credibility, delivering immediate value with free information, capturing their contact information, and having an effective follow-up campaign. So how do you build a presence that overcomes these challenges and serves as an effective tool in your business?

Traffic

Let's look first at the most challenging piece of this puzzle: *traffic*. If you don't have traffic coming to your website, you don't have leads. This is why our company has invested a lot of time, energy, and money not only in building our website, but we also have invested tens of thousands of dollars in testing PPC (pay per click) and SEO strategies. In the process I've been able to identify and learn about the best strategies and tools in the industry.

One of these systems used in our company and with our top students is the SEO Lead System (SLS). We built this software as a research tool and a website builder all in one. We log into the software to research and identify high-quality targeted keywords for sellers and buyers that get a lot of searches each month and have a low number of competing pages. When we identify a term, we use the software to build a highly optimized lead-generation website around that specific term.

These websites are then recognized and indexed by Google, Bing, Yahoo, and other search engines. These sites have been phenomenally successful in showing up on the first page of search engine results, sometimes within days of being built. If you've never applied a successful SEO strategy to a website, then you don't know what an incredible result it can have, a result that many companies spend tens of thousands of dollars to achieve. The best part is that building these sites requires no technical knowledge and can be done by anyone, even if you, like me, have never written a single line of software code.

Let's be honest: a typical investor, ourselves included, doesn't have the time or the desire to learn how to build SEO-friendly websites. That's good, because the last thing you want to do when running a successful real estate business is spend time behind a computer coding pages.

Capturing Leads

Once you start generating traffic to your website, you have to capture the visitors' information. This is where a majority of investors who have implemented a basic online strategy are frequently misguided and fall short on results. This step is all about understanding the importance of and the proper setup of lead-capture sites, which we touched on briefly in Chapter 16.

The overriding goal of a lead-capture site is to give the largest percentage of visitors to your website a reason to leave their information behind before they exit. There are millions of sites online and most visitors jump around from one site to another—with what we refer to as IADD (Internet Attention Deficit Disorder)—and make snap judgments on the site's benefits in the first couple of seconds. That's why it's critical to capture their attention instantly and give an immediate and powerful reason to induce them to leave their information behind so that you have a way to follow up and build a relationship.

The main reason why most investor websites get this step wrong and fail to capture leads is because the lead-capture site is built on information around a specific service or property that an investor wants to market at a particular time. We know this is a recipe for failure, because we constantly study online marketers and have been testing these strategies in our own business for many years.

Instead of focusing on properties or specific services, the most successful investor marketers build their lead-capture strategy around educating prospects and giving away valuable information for free. They share expertise that educates and adds value to website visitors. For example, a site might show visitors the timeline involved in a foreclosure. Or it might let them download for free an e-book explaining "How to Sell Your House in 14 Days or Less." The information is given in return for the visitor's willingness to "opt in" or leave behind their information such as name, e-mail address, and a phone number.

Now you may think, "Great, I have a list of prospects interested in information, but how does it relate to buying and selling homes?" The essence of this strategy is to position yourself as an absolute expert in your local market and to educate your visitor. As a website visitor, it's very easy to find a reason to not leave behind personal information if you are not interested in a specific service or if you don't like something about a specific property. But if you can derive immediate educational value and learn something new about a topic that brought you to the site, you are more likely to leave behind your information.

Whether someone is looking to buy, sell, rent, borrow money, fix a house, or invest in real estate, you want to establish yourself as an authority in the areas in which they are seeking information. This strategy helped us build a huge list of prospects in various areas of real estate, which not only allowed our company to buy, sell, and rent hundreds of properties, but also opened doors to adding multiple streams of income opportunities to our investing business.

In essence, the power of this strategy lies is increasing your influence by building a powerful e-mailing list. The more contacts you have, the greater is your influence, which leads to more business referrals and affiliate opportunities, which result in new income streams. This is a powerful business strategy we teach our coaching students: A website is not just about selling a product; it's about building your influence.

Blogging

The next big piece of the online puzzle is your company blog. It acts as a hub website where you introduce visitors to your company, build credibility, and build an online relationship with prospects. It's a vehicle for continuing the theme of building informational value for visitors by sharing information and free articles. However, unlike lead-capture sites, which are built around the strategy of presenting immediate value to visitors with the sole purpose of capturing their information, your blog is also a chance to showcase your company and your properties, and to emphasize how and why someone can and should do business with you.

The overall site is built on a blogging platform such as WordPress. WordPress is an excellent platform, because most Web developers are familiar with it, so it's easy to find support in creating and maintaining the site. Also, programmers have created thousands of functionality plug-ins that allow you to incorporate video, Web forms, pictures, and other useful tools to websites built on this platform.

The best real estate investor blogs include several elements. The foundation of the site is built on a blog section where you post short articles on topics related to real estate investing. This section—which you should consistently update for strong SEO results—is also the secret behind the effectiveness of the site as it delivers fresh content and provides your visitors a reason to keep coming back. It allows you to stay in front of your prospective customers and build a relationship online so that they think of your company when they are ready to take action on buying, selling, or renting real estate.

A company blog could include other sections: Homes for Sale, where you showcase properties and investment opportunities; Testimonials, which focuses on building your credibility; and finally sections on services your company offers such as Buy a Home, FAQ (Frequently Asked Questions), Sell Your Home, and Investors.

We teach our top students not only how to create a blog, but how to outsource this part of the business by effectively utilizing an army of developers and virtual assistants.

Social Media

Your Web marketing presence would not be complete without social media. You've heard plenty about Facebook, LinkedIn, Twitter, Google+, etc., but how does social media help you make money in the real estate business, and how can you be strategic about your time and efforts?

We believe social media is an absolute *must* for anyone who wants to be competitive online today and in the future. The fact that about a billion people are on Facebook alone is sufficient reason to get started. As the Internet evolves and people change their online habits, you and your business must also adapt to remain relevant.

Another reason to start building your social media presence is that it's the quickest and least-expensive way to put your company on the Internet and to connect with hundreds, if not thousands, of real estate investors and professionals in your niche market—locally and nationally.

The key to leveraging social media is knowing which activities to outsource and which to do yourself. You can outsource generic functions such as designing, posting information about deals your company is offering, or updating events you may be attending. But you want to have a personal touch for other communication, such as greeting contacts or sharing your experiences. You can do this in just a couple of minutes a day.

We have used this social media strategy to enlarge our company's circle of influence. In just a few years of activity on Facebook, Twitter, and LinkedIn, our company's accounts have accumulated several hundreds of thousands of friends, followers, and connections—many of whom became our partners, students, investors, buyers, and sellers—generating millions of dollars in deals. This is the true power of social media.

To view examples of our social media presence, visit us at www.Facebook.com/FlipThisHouse and www.Facebook.com/CTHomesLLC, or follow us on Twitter at www.twitter.com/fortunebuilders and www.twitter/com/cthomesllc.

Database/CRM/E-mail Marketing and Business Automation

The pieces of online presence we described so far don't address the most effective and important part of your activity, which is *follow-up*. This is where a good CRM system and e-mail marketing platform come into play. CRM software, as we touched on previously, allows you to not only input contact information for clients and track correspondence, but also to note things like the client's spouse's name and the type of house they're selling. You can easily retrieve specifics about the client, so you aren't always starting from square one. In addition, a good CRM system enables you to, for example, send an e-mail blast to all the people in foreclosure whom you've spoken to in the past sixty days.

CRM is one piece we wish we brought into our business a lot sooner. Why? Because before we started using a database, we wasted about twelve months of valuable time and energy by not having a place to store information about people who could have been resources in growing our business. Moreover, we missed out on potential buyers and sellers, and had to play a "hustle" game—explaining who we were to establish trust and credibility—every time we were selling another deal.

The lack of a centralized database and the inability to follow up with clients is the No. 1 reason why so many investors struggle and never grow their business beyond the one-deal-at-a-time outfit. Let us give you an example from our own experience. Before we realized the importance of having a system and a CRM, we would go out and meet buyers, sellers, attorneys, contractors, and other important team members.

But in most cases, if we weren't able to find an immediate benefit from the relationship, we would never get any future benefit nor see a return on our networking time. We easily lost more than $200,000 in potential deals in the first twelve months alone, just because we didn't have a good follow-up system. We know this because we researched a few deals that we weren't able to put together and saw them being marketed for sale on MLS at a healthy profit by our competitors.

Another example of the importance of having a CRM is when it comes to selling deals. Before we had an e-mail list and a platform to contact this list, we would have to market each property as if it were the first one we ever tried to sell. This consumed tremendous amounts of time, money, and energy. Today, before we even buy a property, we can look into our database or market the opportunity to those on our e-mail list and find out if there are any potential buyers or interest in the deal. This greatly minimizes our potential risk and allows us to make money on deals that in the past we wouldn't have touched because of doubts about our ability to sell them.

Wrapping It Up

You can see that the success and growth of your business will depend on your ability to quickly adapt to changes and leverage online strategies. Even as we write this book, some tools and strate-gies we mention will change. That is why staying up to date with what is happening in the market is so important.

Now let's find out what Michael has to say about time. ✤

For more information about how we can help you as a real estate investor go to: www.MasteryForInvestors.com.

On the Subject
of Time

Michael E. Gerber

*Take time to deliberate; but when the time for action arrives, stop
thinking and go in.*

—Andrew Jackson

"I'm running out of time!" real estate investors often
lament. "I've got to learn how to manage my time
more carefully!"

Of course, they see no real solution to this problem. They're
just worrying the subject to death. Singing the real estate investor's blues.

Some make a real effort to control time. Maybe they go to time
management classes, or faithfully try to record their activities during
every hour of the day.

But it's hopeless. Even when real estate investors work harder,
even when they keep precise records of their time, there's always a
shortage of it. It's as if they're looking at a square clock in a round

189

universe. Something doesn't fit. The result: the real estate investor is constantly chasing work, money, life.

And the reason is simple. Real estate investors don't see time for what it really is. They think of time with a small "t," rather than Time with a capital "T."

Yet Time is simply another word for your *life*. It's your ultimate asset, your gift at birth—and you can spend it any way you want. Do you know how you want to spend it? Do you have a plan?

How do *you* deal with Time? Are you even conscious of it? If you are, I bet you are constantly locked into either the future or the past. Relying on either memory or imagination.

Do you recognize these voices? "Once I get through this, I can have a drink . . . go on a vacation . . . retire." "I remember when I was young and practicing real estate investment was satisfying."

As you go to bed at midnight, are you thinking about waking up at 7:00 a.m. so that you can get to the office by 8:00 a.m. so that you can go to lunch by noon, because your software people will be there at 1:30 p.m. and you've got a full schedule and a new client scheduled for 2:30 p.m.?

Most of us are prisoners of the future or the past. While pinballing between the two, we miss the richest moments of our life—the present. Trapped forever in memory or imagination, we are strangers to the here and now. Our future is nothing more than an extension of our past, and the present is merely the background.

It's sobering to think that right now each of us is at a precise spot somewhere between the beginning of our Time (our birth) and the end of our Time (our death). No wonder everyone frets about Time. What really terrifies us is that *we're using up our life and we can't stop it.*

It feels as if we're plummeting toward the end with nothing to break our free fall. Time is out of control! Understandably, this is horrifying, mostly because the real issue is not time with a small "t" but Death with a big "D."

From the depths of our existential anxiety, we try to put Time in a different perspective—all the while pretending we can manage it.

We talk about Time as though it were something other than what it is. "Time is money," we announce, as though that explains it.

But what every real estate investor should know is that Time is life. And Time ends! Life ends!

The big, walloping, irresolvable problem is that *we don't know how much Time we have left.*

Do you feel the fear? Do you want to get over it?

Let's look at Time more seriously.

To fully grasp Time with a capital "T," you have to ask the big Question: *How do I wish to spend the rest of my Time?*

Because I can assure you that if you don't ask that big Question with a big "Q," you will forever be assailed by the little questions. You'll shrink the whole of your life to *this time* and *next time* and the *last time*—all the while wondering, *what time is it?*

It's like running around the deck of a sinking ship worrying about where you left the keys to your cabin.

You must accept that you have only so much Time; that you're using up that Time second by precious second. And that your Time, your life, is the most valuable asset you have. Of course, you can use your Time any way you want. But unless you choose to use it as richly, as rewardingly, as excitingly, as intelligently, as *intentionally* as possible, you'll squander it and fail to appreciate it.

Indeed, if you are oblivious to the value of your Time, you'll commit the single greatest sin: You will live your life unconscious of its passing you by.

Until you deal with Time with a capital "T," you'll worry about time with a small "t" until you have no Time—or life—left. Then your Time will be history . . . along with your life.

I can anticipate the question: If Time is the problem, why not just take on fewer clients? Well, that's certainly an option, but probably not necessary. I know a real estate investor with a small company who sees four times as many clients as the average, yet the he and his staff don't work long hours. How is it possible?

This real estate investor has a system. By using this expert system, the employees can do everything the real estate investor or his team members would do—everything that isn't real estate investor-dependent.

Be versus Do

Remember when we all asked, "What do I want to be when I grow up?" It was one of our biggest concerns as children.

Notice that the question isn't, "What do I want to *do* when I grow up?" It's "What do I want to *be?*"

Shakespeare wrote, "To be or not to be." Not "To do or not to do."

But when you grow up, people always ask you, "What do you *do?*" How did the question change from *being* to *doing?* How did we miss the critical distinction between the two?

Even as children, we sensed the distinction. The real question we were asking was not what we would end up *doing* when we grew up, but who we would *be*.

We were talking about a *life* choice, not a *work* choice. We instinctively saw it as a matter of how we spend our Time, not what we do in time.

Look to children for guidance. I believe that as children we instinctively saw Time as life and tried to use it wisely. As children, we wanted to make a life choice, not a work choice. As children, we didn't know—or care—that work had to be done on time, on budget.

Until you see Time for what it really is—your life span—you will always ask the wrong question.

Until you embrace the whole of your Time and shape it accordingly, you will never be able to fully appreciate the moment.

Until you fully appreciate every second that comprises Time, you will never be sufficiently motivated to live those seconds fully.

Until you're sufficiently motivated to live those seconds fully, you will never see fit to change the way you are. You will never take the quality and sanctity of Time seriously.

And unless you take the sanctity of Time seriously, you will continue to struggle to catch up with something behind you. Your frustrations will mount as you try to snatch the second that just whisked by.

If you constantly fret about time with a small "t," then Time will blow right past you. And you'll miss the whole point, the real truth about Time: You can't manage it; you never could. You can only *live* it.

And so that leaves you with these questions: How do I live my life? How do I give significance to it? How can I be here now, in this moment?

Once you begin to ask these questions, you'll find yourself moving toward a much fuller, richer life. But if you continue to be caught up in the banal work you do every day, you're never going to find the time to take a deep breath, exhale, and be present in the now.

So, let's talk about the subject of *work*. But first, let's find out what Than and Paul have to say about time. ✤

www.michaelegerber.com/co-author

CHAPTER

22

Time Is Your Most Valuable Asset

Than Merrill
Paul Esajian

Lost time is never found again.

—Proverb

Time is your most valuable asset. You've certainly heard this statement before from many successful people. But do you ever pause to try to understand why this is commonly shared wisdom? What does this statement really mean? How does it relate to real estate investors? What does it mean to you personally?

Remember the next time you plan on being late, or waste someone's time: more than any asset, money or property, time is irreplaceable. Respect it. Cherish it.

Most importantly, if time is truly our most valuable asset, how do we better organize, manage, and invest it? In this chapter, we will address some of these questions, and we'll share a few practical solutions for achieving better returns on your time investments so that you can grow your real estate empire!

Lifestyle Design

Let's look at why time is such an important resource for so many people. We continually coach new real estate investors across the country. It is amazing to see how many of these investors decide to abandon their successful, high-earning professional careers for the opportunity to own their time.

We've observed that the main factor driving most people toward starting a real estate investment business is rooted not in money but in freedom of time and in lifestyle design. This means different things to different people. For some, lifestyle design implies spending more time with family and children, while for others it's traveling the world, devoting more time to charitable causes, or simply being more passionate about what they do every day. No matter the purpose, freedom of time and lifestyle design are usually the underlying motivators for change. Yet despite it all, many real estate investors end up struggling to achieve these goals because of deeply ingrained misconceptions and years of bad habits about how to approach and value time.

Create Income from Wealth, Not Work

From an early age, most of us were taught to trade time for money. Likewise, if we wanted to get ahead or make more money, we were told to get a second job and to trade more time for money. Or we were taught to get an education or a specialized degree so that we would increase our probability of getting a better job where we would earn more money for our time. Think about it: Do top lawyers trade time for money? What about doctors? The truth is most people trade time for money. We think we have all been brainwashed.

The truth is, however, that extremely wealthy people do not trade time for money. Truly affluent people let their assets do all the heavy lifting, while they spend less time working each year. Wealthy people create income from their wealth, not their work.

Their wealth creation continues, regardless of whether they are at work, on vacation, or asleep in bed.

So how do you move from being part of the lower or middle class, and gain membership into this more-affluent group? There are several options for you to ensure your upward mobility, but your probability of success is dramatically enhanced by the production of entrepreneurial income beyond what you earn at a typical 9-to-5 job. In other words, you have to continually acquire assets and make investments that produce wealth for you.

A lot of people pursue a real estate investing career because they want to acquire assets and because there is no ceiling as to what you can earn. However, for most people, real estate investing becomes just another high-paying job if you don't build systems for your business.

The goal should be to use your knowledge of the business to create short-term income-flipping properties and then roll that money into longer-term assets that produce passive income. Flipping properties will require a major time investment until you build systems in your business. Once those systems are built, your business can produce income without you.

Therefore, you should constantly strive to reinvent yourself and your business so that every day your income becomes less dependent on your "personal" time. A true real estate entrepreneur does not trade time for money. All ultra-successful real estate investors build businesses, while others trade time for money. Once you make a mental shift and start understanding and working toward this model, your business and your income can grow exponentially.

Leveraging Knowledge and Time

How do we get to the point of owning more of our time? Once you acknowledge and commit to rejecting the idea of trading time for money, the process of owning more of your time becomes straightforward. The shortest path to get there is leveraging the time and knowledge of other successful real estate investors and business people who have created sustainable business models.

Surround yourself with, study, and emulate people who have done it. When you spend time with the most successful and wealthy investors, you start learning that you must think very differently than an average working individual who simply trades time for money. Successful real estate investors realize that it takes a lot of time to build a business, but it doesn't always have to be their time.

Taking Control of Time

The first step in better leveraging other people's time is to understand where and how you currently use your own time. You can begin this process by keeping a detailed journal about where you commit and spend your time over the course of a two-day period. Simply recording what you do in fifteen-minute increments over a two-day period will give you a very complete picture of how efficient you are with your time. Then you need to analyze how you are spending your time and how much of that time is spent on "income-producing" activities.

This exercise is very simplistic and very revealing. Everyone who does it for the first time realizes how much time he or she wastes each and every day. When you add up that time over the course of a month or a year, the waste becomes enormous.

Identifying your time inefficiencies is part of the reason for going through this exercise. It requires some commitment, but it's an essential process. Until you have a clearer picture of how you are currently using your time, it's difficult to begin the process of valuing, controlling, outsourcing, and eventually owning your time.

The next step is to understand and begin to apply the 80/20 rule to your investment business. First, list all the activities you do in your business. Highlight the top 20 percent of those activities that contribute to driving income and increasing revenues. These include planning and systemizing marketing, meeting with sellers, meeting with buyers, creating systems to drive revenue, raising money, strategic networking, and recruiting and training staff. If you are a beginner investor, you will be wearing many additional hats, but your goal should always be to spend as much time driving revenue as possible.

Next, examine the remaining 80 percent of activities. As we discuss below, you'll want to place a value next to each one and think about whom you could outsource those activities to. We divide these activities into three categories: low-, mid-, and high-wage replacement activities.

1. Low-Wage Replacement Activities

These are things you do on a daily basis that could easily be outsourced to a personal assistant, virtual assistant, or in some cases a housekeeper. Low-wage replacement activities are the bottom 20 percent of activities that have more to do with personal living and personal organization. These would include things like cleaning your house, doing laundry, running errands, shopping for office supplies, checking mail, filing, etc. These activities do not create revenue for your business. These are the activities you have to outsource first so you can have more time. With a little training, a personal assistant could handle these tasks for $10 to $15 per hour.

When you outsource these jobs, you will free up a lot of time that can be dedicated to improving your business. When we did this exercise for the first time, we were shocked at how much time we were spending each week on these types of activities.

We recommend you do this right away, even if you haven't found your first real estate deal yet. Have enough confidence that your time is more valuable than running errands and cleaning your house. When you do this, you will have more time to study the business well and increase your knowledge base. If you don't have reserves, do this as soon as you can after you complete your first deal.

2. Mid-Wage Replacement Activities

As you evaluate how you use your time as a real estate investor, you will realize that many things you do every day could be outsourced to someone by paying $15 to $40 an hour. In most cases, investors will find that 40 percent of their time is spent executing tasks that could be outsourced to others in this mid-wage pay scale.

These are usually technician- and managerial-type activities that don't generate direct revenue. Many investors have a hard time letting go of these tasks, including research and acquisitions, rehab management, sales screening and management, property management, bookkeeping, IT, and Web work.

When you outsource these activities, you will free up a massive amount of time for yourself, which will allow you to focus more of your time on income-generating activities. At what point do you know you can hire someone to do these activities? It's when your business has enough sales opportunities to produce income that will double or triple the amount you spend on hiring someone to do back-end work. Your goal is to focus your working time on the highest income-generating activities. This will free you up to relax and enjoy other areas of your life.

3. High-Wage Replacement Activities

The next 20 percent of activities in your business are composed of professional services and high-level managerial activities. These activities usually can be outsourced to specialists at $40 to $150 per hour. Some of the tasks that fit into this category are done by attorneys, accountants, and tax advisors, and you will outsource these tasks for a long time. Others include experienced marketers who can keep growing your business opportunities, experienced acquisition managers and sales people, and anyone who can help you recruit, train, and manage people effectively.

A few of these team members should also be able to drive revenue, so commission structures are not uncommon in this area.

As mentioned before, our benchmark for hiring people on commission is whether they can generate revenue that's three times what they get paid.

Having a breakdown of the types of activities in your business, an understanding of where you spend your time, and a way to balance this equation are excellent steps in the exercise of leveraging time to produce results. It's an exercise that we do twice a year in our business.

If you would like to find out more about how we've set up our office, business, and train other investors, please visit www. MasteryForInvestors.com.

Time Blocking

This is another strategy we use in conquering time by getting more done in less time. Time blocking is a strategy for finishing more projects and improving systems in your business so more parts of it can be automated. Instead of reacting to what happens in your daily life and business, you take control and start strategically deciding where you commit your time on a daily and weekly basis. Time blocking takes some planning and commitment, but it produces results very quickly.

Here is an example of a time-blocking system we use and teach. We always set our weekly goals on Sunday evenings. Notice that we don't do it on Mondays, because (1) we want to be at full speed starting the week, and (2) chances are our lives and business will get so busy that we'll get caught up in a reactive mode versus planned execution. During the week, we chunk our time into average segments of sixty minutes, with five- to ten-minute breaks in between. We use the breaks to respond to e-mails and phone calls or to catch up with other immediate issues. We might also plan for thirty- to ninety-minute segments, depending on a project. This allows us to move forward on our business day, with few interruptions.

A few other points: we limit our goals to no more than six projects per day, so we can stay focused. And we don't allow overflow on projects or add new noncritical projects until the ones we set out to accomplish are completed.

Wrapping It Up

All the strategies described in this chapter will help you grow a business that requires less of your time and allows you to design the life of your dreams. Without a doubt, a lot of these strategies require discipline and a commitment to weekly implementation. But this is a small sacrifice to make if you keep in mind the ultimate goal of building an amazing business in which you own your time!

Now, let's read what Michael has to say about work. ✤

For more information about how we can help you as a real estate investor go to: www.MasteryForInvestors.com.

CHAPTER
23

On the Subject of Work

Michael E. Gerber

As we learn we always change, and so our perception. This changed perception then becomes a new Teacher inside each of us.

—Hyemeyohsts Storm

In the business world, as the saying goes, the entrepreneur knows something about everything, the technician knows everything about something, and the telephone operator just knows everything.

In a real estate investment company, real estate investors see their natural work as the work of the technician. The Supreme Technician. Often to the exclusion of everything else.

After all, real estate investors get zero preparation working as a manager and spend no time thinking as an entrepreneur—those just aren't courses offered in today's schools of real estate investment. By the time they own their own real estate investment company, they're just doing it, doing it, doing it.

At the same time, they want everything—freedom, respect, money. Most of all, they want to rid themselves of meddling bosses and start their own company. That way they can be their own boss and take home all the money. These real estate investors are in the throes of an entrepreneurial seizure.

Real estate investors who have been praised for their ability to handle difficult acquisitions or their extensive knowledge of rehab management believe they have what it takes to run a real estate investment company. It's not unlike the plumber who becomes a contractor because he's a great plumber. Sure, he may be a great plumber . . . but it doesn't necessarily follow that he knows how to build a company that does this work.

It's the same for a real estate investor. So many of them are surprised to wake up one morning and discover that they're nowhere near as equipped for owning their own company as they thought they were.

More than any other subject, work is the cause of obsessive-compulsive behavior by real estate investors.

Work. You've got to do it every single day.

Work. If you fall behind, you'll pay for it.

Work. There's either too much or not enough.

So many real estate investors describe work as what they do when they're busy. Some discriminate between the work they *could* be doing as real estate investors and the work they *should* be doing as real estate investors.

But according to the E-Myth, they're exactly the same thing. The work you *could* do and the work you *should* do as a real estate investor are identical. Let me explain.

Strategic Work versus Tactical Work

Real estate investors can do only two kinds of work: strategic work and tactical work.

Tactical work is easier to understand, because it's what almost every real estate investor does almost every minute of every hour of every day. It's called getting the job done. It's called doing business.

Tactical work includes filing, billing, answering the telephone, inspecting property, screening sales, handling media advertising services, going to the bank, arranging for financing, and seeing clients.

The E-Myth says that tactical work is all the work real estate investors find themselves doing in a real estate investment company to *avoid* doing the strategic work.

"I'm too busy," most real estate investors will tell you.

"How come nothing goes right unless I do it myself?" they complain in frustration.

Real estate investors say these things when they're up to their ears in tactical work. But most real estate investors don't understand that if they had done more strategic work, they would have less tactical work to do.

Real estate investors are doing strategic work when they ask the following questions:

- Why am I a real estate investor?
- What will my company look like when it's done?
- What must my company look, act, and feel like in order for it to compete successfully?
- What are the key indicators of my company?

Please note that I said real estate investors ask these questions when they are doing strategic work. I didn't say these are the questions they necessarily answer.

That is the fundamental difference between strategic work and tactical work. Tactical work is all about *answers:* How to do this. How to do that.

Strategic work, in contrast, is all about *questions:* What company are we really in? Why are we in that company? Who specifically is our company determined to serve? When will I sell this company? How and where will this company be doing business when I sell it? And so forth.

Not that strategic questions don't have answers. Real estate investors who commonly ask strategic questions know that once they ask such a question, they're already on their way to *envisioning* the answer. Question and answer are part of a whole. You can't find the right answer until you've asked the right question.

Tactical work is much easier, because the question is always more obvious. In fact, you don't ask the tactical question; instead, the question arises from a result you need to get or a problem you need to solve. Billing a client is tactical work. Advising a client is tactical work. Firing an employee is tactical work. Conducting a property analysis is tactical work.

Tactical work is the stuff you do every day in your company. Strategic work is the stuff you plan to do to create an exceptional company/business/enterprise.

In tactical work, the question comes from *out there* rather than *in here*. The tactical question is about something *outside* of you, whereas the strategic question is about something *inside* of you.

The tactical question is about something you *need* to do, whereas the strategic question is about something you *want* to do. Want versus need.

If tactical work consumes you,

- you are always reacting to something outside of you;
- your company runs you, you don't run it;
- your employees run you, you don't run them; and
- your life runs you, you don't run your life.

You must understand that the more strategic work you do, the more intentional your decisions, your company, and your life become. *Intention* is the byword of strategic work.

Everything on the outside begins to serve you, to serve your vision, rather than forcing you to serve it. Everything you *need* to do is congruent with what you want to do. It means you have a vision, an aim, a purpose, a strategy, an *envisioned* result.

Strategic work is the work you do to *design* your company, to design your life.

Tactical work is the work you do to *implement* the design created by strategic work.

Without strategic work, there is no design. Without strategic work, all that's left is keeping busy.

There's only one thing left to do. It's time to take action. But first, let's read what Than and Paul have to say on the subject of work. ✤

www.michaelegerber.com/co-author

CHAPTER 24

Working Smarter
... Not Harder

Than Merrill
Paul Esajian

(Work is) something made greater by ourselves and in turn that makes us greater.

—Maya Angelou

A common misconception is that successful real estate investors do not work. Instead, they are known for seeking out opportunities and investing capital to generate returns. Yet anyone who has successfully invested in real estate knows that there is a lot of work behind putting a successful investment or deal together. There is even more work if you want to build a business out of it.

Without putting in hard work, investments can turn into huge risks and real estate businesses can fail. The good news is that we do have a choice in how we approach this work and can make it more enjoyable and rewarding. We do this by embracing what is called the "Working Smarter . . . Not Harder" principles.

Resistance

In his very insightful book *Do the Work*, Steven Pressfield covers the principles of resistance and how they affect our everyday work. He writes: "Rule of Thumb: The more important a call or action is to our soul's evolution, the more Resistance we will feel toward pursuing it." What Steven means is that the moment you decide to take action on something important, you must expect challenges.

In real estate, this means that as soon as you set an investing or business goal, you will experience every form of resistance to achieving it. Yet you must press forward, because your soul's evolution depends on you striving to achieve that goal. Pressfield explains that resistance is a natural companion of work, and he provides tools to overcome this resistance. In real estate, our tools include strategies to reach our goals and grow successful businesses by "Working Smarter . . . Not Harder."

In business, as in life, the greatest resistance you will have to work is doing it. That first step of putting our efforts in motion to produce a result or a desired outcome is what causes us the most anxiety and consumes our energy. This is not because real estate investors are lazy. On the contrary, most investors have an abundance of energy and excitement for the business. The resistance usually comes from the fear of the unknown, which is part of any real estate deal.

You can easily overcome such paralysis, however, by surrounding yourself with other investors and mentors who are active in the business. Why? Because it's a lot easier to succeed in situations when you are stumped if you have the confidence to move forward by knowing that others will help and that you can reach out for an answer. The most successful real estate investors always have a strong network of professionals and other successful investors. Access to the right information is just one example of "Working Smarter . . . Not Harder."

Strengths and Weaknesses

Another way we can utilize the strategies of "Working Smarter . . . Not Harder" is by understanding our personal strengths and weaknesses. As we already covered in Chapter 22, time is the most-valuable asset for any real estate investor. So, a key strategy is to spend as much time as you can on leveraging your strengths and hiring people who can fill the gaps in areas of your weaknesses.

For example, if you have a very strong sales background but you are weak in systems and technology, you should not be spending several hours a day building online systems for your business. Instead, you and your business will be much better off hiring someone who has strength in this area. Similarly, if you are strong on technology but lack sales skills, you are not going to be putting yourself in a position to win if you are the one trying to negotiate deals.

We strongly suggest that you and any of your work associates should take a personality test, if you haven't already, so you can determine your strengths and most suitable job traits. You can do an online search to find all kinds of personality tests, but our favorite is DISC, developed by John Geier. Than took the DISC test years ago and found it very insightful; he was strongest in a visionary, leadership role. We believe the more you understand yourself, the better you can communicate and work with others. Likewise, if you understand your weaknesses, you can add other people who have those strengths to your team.

As mentioned before, we also suggest you include personality testing as part of the application process when hiring employees. That way, you can add team members who offset some of your weaknesses and create a stronger overall team for the business.

Looking back, we realize one of the reasons our real estate business was able to grow so quickly was because we built a team made up of individuals who each excelled in different areas.

Building Systems

Building systems, which we have discussed in multiple chapters, is another example of "Working Smarter . . . Not Harder." This principle is a central message of the E-Myth philosophy and has been an inspiration and a driving force behind the growth of thousands of businesses, including mine. Systems enable work to be done more efficiently. Without systems you are always working harder, because every time you take on an activity in your investment business, there is no road map to complete it.

Because you are reading this book, we know we don't have to spend much more time in convincing you of the benefits of creating systems in your business. However, ask yourself how effective you have been in applying these systems in your investment business. The truth is the majority of investors are not great at it. And I'd venture to say that's because they were never exposed to a process for creating these systems in their business.

Systems have enabled us to scale and build a business in which someone new to real estate investing can be hired and trained very quickly to take over responsibility in important parts of our business. These systems are also a foundation of what we share with and use to teach our coaching students.

Technology

Technology and automation are essential to "Working Smarter . . . Not Harder" principles. Technology can be a great accelerator when building a real estate business. From marketing to research, from client management to follow-up to team training, our business wouldn't be where it is today without technology. So why are so many investors slow to fully embrace it? In our experience, that's because they don't understand how influential and helpful it can be in their business and personal lives. Another reason is because investors rarely commit truly to applying the principles of "Strengths and Weaknesses."

In our business, we constantly seek out ways to use technology to help automate activities, minimize risk, and maximize returns on our investments. One of the main tools we use to automate marketing and follow-up is our real estate industry CRM (customer relationship management), as discussed in Chapter 20. Because this system combines our online presence and connects leads generated from online and offline marketing by depositing them into a central location, the follow-up and transition from one department to another is virtually seamless. Undoubtedly, this saves hundreds of hours of work time for our team every year and results in more deals being closed due to improved and automated follow-up. It also ensures a much better experience for people who do business with our company because all our customer information is well-organized and easy to access.

Another tool we've embraced in order to boost work efficiency is a virtual phone system. With its limitless extension and transfer possibilities, this system has helped create a professional presence for our business and has given us the flexibility to take calls in the office, in the field, at home, or while traveling. It also can be used as a great extension of your marketing through voice-mail boxes and extension tracking for a better understanding of which marketing methods produce the best results. Lastly, the system doubles as an eFax system, which deposits faxes right in our team's e-mail inbox.

There are a couple of other tools worth mentioning. One is Google Apps, at www.google.com/a, which we use for e-mail communication, shared calendars, shared documents, and chat. This allows for much easier and effective communication with customers and between team members. The other tool we live by is Dropbox, at www.Dropbox.com, which acts as a virtual storage of all our electronic files and lets us easily update and share with our entire team across different devices and computers.

We'd also like to share some of the tools we use for building systems that train our employees. We've already touched on the mind-mapping process, which we use to train new employees in processes. We also offer a lot of online trainings and videos to help continually improve and grow our team. The software program we use to capture and edit training videos is Camtasia at www.TechSmith.com. We also use tools that allow us to expand the geographic boundaries of our business and have virtual employees. Skype, at www.skype.com, gives us free phone and video calls worldwide, while GoToMeeting, at www.gotomeeting.com, enables us to share computer screens with team members located anywhere with the help of an Internet connection. We use these tools to conduct video meetings and online trainings.

We post our training videos to our internal training center. This center is used for everything from new hire trainings to ongoing employee education. It is one of the best tools we built, because anytime we hire team members, the center enables them to get up and running very quickly. Within the training center, we created a curriculum of classes categorized by employee position. We also have our employees contribute to this training center so it is a continuously evolving library of training material for future hires.

All the technology mentioned in this section is easily accessible and relatively inexpensive for a small-business owner. If used and leveraged well, these tools can lead to more closed deals and more work completed in the least amount of time, allowing you more freedom and flexibility to enjoy the real estate investor lifestyle.

Wrapping It Up

This chapter covers a few examples of how you can "Work Smarter . . . Not Harder" in your real estate investment business. By embracing these principles, the goal is to create a work environment for you and your team members that eliminates many of the negatives of tedious work, while greatly increasing your chances of success. Building a successful real estate company requires commitment and a lot of work. If your goal is to create a lasting business, you need to be smart about it and enjoy the process.

Work smart; work hard. And, as Michael's about to tell you, take action! ✤

For more information about how we can help you as a real estate investor go to: www.MasteryForInvestors.com.

On the Subject of Taking Action

Michael E. Gerber

Deliberation is the work of many men. Action, of one alone.
—Charles de Gaulle

I t's time to get started, time to take action. Time to stop thinking about the old company and start thinking about the new company. It's not a matter of coming up with better companies; it's about reinventing the business of real estate investment.

And the real estate investor has to take personal responsibility for it.

That's you.

So sit up and pay attention!

You, the real estate investor, have to be interested. You cannot abdicate accountability for the business of real estate investment, the administration of real estate investment, or the finance of real estate investment.

Although the goal is to create systems into which real estate investors can plug reasonably competent people—systems that allow

217

the company to run without them—real estate investors must take responsibility for that happening.

I can hear the chorus now: "But we're real estate investors! We shouldn't have to know about this." To that I say: whatever. If you don't give a flip about your company, fine—close your mind to new knowledge and accountability. But if you want to succeed, then you'd better step up and take responsibility, and you'd better do it now.

All too often, real estate investors take no responsibility for the business of real estate investment but instead delegate tasks without any understanding of what it takes to do them; without any interest in what their people are actually doing; without any sense of what it feels like to be at the front desk when a client comes in and has to wait for forty-five minutes; and without any appreciation for the entity that is creating their livelihood.

Real estate investors can open the portals of change in an instant. All you have to do is say, "I don't want to do it that way anymore." Saying it will begin to set you free—even though you don't yet understand what the company will look like after it's been reinvented.

This demands an intentional leap from the known into the unknown. It further demands that you live there—in the unknown—for a while. It means discarding the past, everything you once believed to be true.

Think of it as soaring rather than plunging.

Thought Control

You should now be clear about the need to organize your thoughts first, and then your business. Because the organization of your thoughts is the foundation for the organization of your business.

If we try to organize our business without organizing our thoughts, we will fail to attack the problem.

We have seen that organization is not simply time management. Nor is it people management. Nor is it tidying up desks or alphabetizing client files. Organization is first, last, and always cleaning up the mess of our minds.

By learning how to *think* about the practice of real estate investment, by learning how to *think* about your priorities, and by learning how to *think* about your life, you'll prepare yourself to do righteous battle with the forces of failure.

Right thinking leads to right action—and now is the time to take action. Because it is only through action that you can translate thoughts into movement in the real world, and, in the process, find fulfillment.

So, first *think* about what you want to do. Then *do* it. Only in this way will you be fulfilled.

How do you put the principles we've discussed in this book to work in your real estate investment company? To find out, accompany me down the path once more:

1. *Create a story about your company.* Your story should be an idealized version of your real estate investment company, a vision of what the preeminent real estate investor in your field should be and why. Your story must become the very heart of your company. It must become the spirit that mobilizes it, as well as everyone who walks through the doors. Without this story, your company will be reduced to plain work.

2. *Organize your company so that it breathes life into your story.* Unless your company can faithfully replicate your story in action, it all becomes fiction. In that case, you'd be better off not telling your story at all. And without a story, you'd be better off leaving your company the way it is and just hoping for the best.

Here are some tips for organizing your real estate investment company:

- Identify the key functions of your company.
- Identify the essential processes that link those functions.

- Identify the results you have determined your company will produce.
- Clearly state in writing how each phase will work.

Take it step by step. Think of your company as a program, a piece of software, a system. It is a collaboration, a collection of processes dynamically interacting with one another.

Of course, your company is also people.

3. *Engage your people in the process.* Why is this the third step rather than the first? Because, contrary to the advice most business experts will give you, you must never engage your people in the process until you yourself are clear about what you intend to do.

The need for consensus is a disease of today's addled mind. It's a product of our troubled and confused times. When people don't know what to believe in, they often ask others to tell them. To ask is not to lead but to follow.

The prerequisite of sound leadership is first to know where you wish to go.

And so, "What do I want?" becomes the first question; not, "What do they want?" In your own company, the vision must first be yours. To follow another's vision is to abdicate your personal accountability, your leadership role, your true power.

In short, the role of leader cannot be delegated or shared. And without leadership, no real estate investment company will ever succeed.

Despite what you have been told, win-win is a secondary step, not a primary one. The opposite of win-win is not necessarily they lose.

Let's say "they" can win by choosing a good horse. The best choice will not be made by consensus. "Guys, what horse do you think we should ride?" will always lead to endless and worthless discussions. By the time you're done jawing, the horse will have already left the post.

Before you talk to your people about what you intend to do in your company and why you intend to do it, you need to reach agreement with yourself.

It's important to know (1) exactly what you want, (2) how you intend to proceed, (3) what's important to you and what isn't, and (4) what you want the company to be and how you want it to get there.

Once you have that agreement, it's critical that you engage your people in a discussion about what you intend to do and why. Be clear—both with yourself and with them.

The Story

The story is paramount because it is your vision. Tell it with passion and conviction. Tell it with precision. Never hurry a great story. Unveil it slowly. Don't mumble or show embarrassment. Never apologize or display false modesty. Look your audience in the eyes and tell your story as though it is the most important one they'll ever hear about business. Your business. The business into which you intend to pour your heart, your soul, your intelligence, your imagination, your time, your money, and your sweaty persistence.

Get into the storytelling zone. Behave as though it means everything to you. Show no equivocation when telling your story.

These tips are important because you're going to tell your story over and over—to clients, to new and old employees, to real estate investors, to team members, and to your family and friends. You're going to tell it at your church or synagogue, to your card-playing or fishing buddies, and to organizations such as Kiwanis, Rotary, YMCA, Hadassah, and Boy Scouts.

There are few moments in your life when telling a great story about a great business is inappropriate.

If it is to be persuasive, you must love your story. Do you think Walt Disney loved his Disneyland story? Or Ray Kroc his McDonald's story? What about Dave Smith at Federal Express? Or Debbie Fields at Mrs. Fields Cookies? Or Tom Watson Jr. at IBM?

Do you think these people loved their stories? Do you think others loved (and still love) to hear them? I daresay all successful entrepreneurs have loved the story of their business. Because that's what true entrepreneurs do. They tell stories that come to life in the form of their business.

Remember: A great story never fails. A great story is always a joy to hear.

In summary, you first need to clarify, both for yourself and for your people, the story of your company. Then you need to detail the process your company must go through to make your story become reality.

I call this the business development process. Others call it reengineering, continuous improvement, reinventing your company, or total quality management.

Whatever you call it, you must take three distinct steps to succeed:

- *Innovation.* Continue to find better ways of doing what you do.
- *Quantification.* Once that is achieved, quantify the impact of these improvements on your company.
- *Orchestration.* Once these improvements are verified, orchestrate this better way of running your company so that it becomes your standard, to be repeated time and again.

In this way, the system works—no matter who's using it. And you've built a company that works consistently, predictably, systematically. A company you can depend on to operate exactly as promised, every single time.

Your vision, your people, your process—all linked.

A superior real estate investment company is a creation of your imagination, a product of your mind. So fire it up and get started! Now let's find out what Than and Paul have to say about taking action. ✤

www.michaelegerber.com/co-author

CHAPTER 26

Attacking Life

Than Merrill
Paul Esajian

Attack life, take risks, and live with unbridled passion. Otherwise you will look back on your life with regret.

—Anonymous

We believe that many people mistakenly believe that extremely successful people have some special gift, talent, or innate skill. Yet when you take a closer look, the special gifts that extremely successful people have is their ability to consistently take action.

Enormously successful people have figured out how to associate massive pain with procrastination and the inability to make decisions. They often have found a way to become very comfortable being uncomfortable. Likewise, successful people also realize that when they do fail, they will learn from those failures and apply that knowledge to their future decisions.

We also believe that anyone can train themselves to think and act like extremely successful people, if they are willing to embrace change at all levels in their lives. Over the years we have become self-development junkies and have made it a consistent practice to surround ourselves with other successful entrepreneurs and business owners. We have also spent considerable time studying some of the top athletes, musicians, and entrepreneurs in an effort to understand why some people succeed and others fail.

In this chapter we share with you some of our insights and discoveries. These observations or "rules" that successful people use to govern their lives have helped us make many major shifts in my own life and will hopefully help you, too, in your business pursuits.

Rule 1: Associate Massive Pain with Bad Habits

Our lives are governed by pain and pleasure. These governors determine what actions we take on a daily basis. Everything we do is to create pleasure or avoid pain. And it's not so much that we're governed by pleasure and pain, as much as we're governed by our perception of what is pleasurable and what is painful.

For example a lot of people want to lose weight, but they don't want to work out. They associate a lot of pain with the thought of working out. Likewise, they often associate pleasure with sitting on the couch and watching TV. Do you see the problem? Their perception of pain and pleasure is being improperly governed.

Yet, most of us know that working out isn't all that painful. In fact, many people can't function if they don't work out on a daily basis. So what is the difference? People who are fit have learned to associate pleasure with the process of working out and pain with not exercising. These people have flip-flopped their pain and pleasure governors.

This same principle can be applied to any bad habit or area of your life that you are looking to change. For example, when Than was in his early twenties and starting his business, he often had a problem with getting things done. He would find any distraction and would only perform when he was under a deadline. Over the years, he completely changed that habit by setting daily goals in the morning and then associating massive pain with not accomplishing those tasks. He literally beats himself up mentally now, if for some reason he wastes time during the day and doesn't accomplish his goals. Likewise, he learned to use the pain-and-pleasure principle to change many of the habits that held him back.

Rule 2: Check Your Ego

You also have to check your ego if you want to grow. We learned about this when we let it hinder our personal growth early on in our careers. In our second year of business, we got involved in a deal where we ended up losing a significant amount of money, because we had too many projects going on at once. We believe we let our egos get in the way of our decision-making process—we thought we knew more then we actually did. It was a hard lesson to learn, but one that ultimately has paid dividends over the years.

When you think you know it all, you often stop listening and stymie your growth. Successful people are always emptying their proverbial cup so they can continually fill it up with new knowledge. They realize they will never know everything and they continually associate pleasure with learning and staying current with market trends.

The real estate market is not static. In fact, it is highly dynamic, so you have to stay in tune with legislative policies, market trends, and new business practices if you want to continue growing on an annual basis.

Rule 3: Value Education

If we were to write you a check for $20,000 right now, many of you would be very happy that you got to this chapter in the book! But for a lot of people, $20,000 wouldn't last through the month. For some people, it literally wouldn't last through the week— that money would come and go, like for lottery winners and their winnings, because they never had the financial education to manage their financial success. So what's more valuable—the money or the financial education?

We will let you answer the question. Would you rather have the money ($20,000) or would you rather have the education of how to consistently make $20,000 for the rest of your life?

If you took billionaire investor Warren Buffett's money from him and set him loose in a brand-new industry and a brand-new career, there is very strong probability that he would earn tens of millions in a short period of time because of his accumulated investment education.

So what is the difference between a business icon like Buffet and the average person? It is education. Ask yourself what would you rather have—money that can be fleeting or a financial education that can produce a lifetime of wealth?

Rule 4: Build for the Long Term

Growing a real estate business can be very profitable, but money is meaningless if you never have the time for the more important aspects of your life. We have met many real estate investors with decades of investment experience who still work more than fifty hours a week. That's why it is so important to acquire more than just real estate-specific knowledge. That knowledge will prepare you to do deals, but you still will be trading your time for money. Business-specific knowledge will allow you to translate your real estate knowledge into a systems-centric business that is not dependent on you.

When you take a systems-centric approach to building your business, you have to be prepared to make less money initially than you would if you were to just focus on doing deals in your first six months. That's because a lot of your time will be spent preparing your business for growth by creating standard operating procedures and implementing systems.

However, your patience will prove to be a virtue shortly thereafter because your business will be a lot more profitable when the systems are set up to evaluate deals quicker and handle more volume.

Plus, you will be setting your business up so that it is not completely dependent on your time. Ultimately, that is the philosophy of this entire book.

Rule 5: Develop a High Level of Self-Accountability

We have observed that extremely successful people learn to develop a high level of self-accountability and a strong belief that they are in complete control of their personal and financial destiny. They believe internal forces control their life. These internal forces, like the choices they make and their own efforts, ultimately control their life. They see a direct link between their actions and the likelihood of getting positive results in their lives. They always point the finger at themselves as opposed to blaming others.

On the other end of the spectrum are people who believe external forces shape their destiny. These people believe that fate, other people, their upbringing, the economy, and luck control their destiny. People who let external factors rule their lives often feel victimized and don't see a link between their actions and the results they get. They are often easily swayed by the opinions of others, and generally there is a lot of blame going on in their world. They attribute any successes or failures to luck rather than their own efforts.

How can you make a change so you are less likely to blame external forces? The first thing you should do is consistently set daily and or weekly goals. When you chunk things down it is easier to create small victories that create momentum in your life. You should then reward yourself for achieving these weekly goals so you constantly reinforce positive belief patterns that are linked to your decisions and personal efforts. Through this practice you are more likely to take responsibility and accountability for the choices you make.

Likewise, it is very important to buy into the power of personal development and education. When you develop a personal development path, you will put yourself through a process of self-realization that will help you develop positive habits.

Rule 6: Always Keep Your "Why" in Focus

We talked about this concept at the beginning of this book. Obviously, what you do is real estate investing and how you do it is through the process of flipping homes, but you really need to think about "why" you want to be in this business. And if you are already active, what is your *why*? If you don't understand what your *why* is, then you're not going have a passion that lights up your life and keeps you going months down the road when you get caught up in a deal that's blowing up in your face.

After you've accomplished two to three deals, you may find yourself lacking motivation if you don't constantly reconnect back to your why. What is it that is driving you to get to where you want? Whatever it is, you need to define it before moving forward.

Rule 7: Live Without Regrets

Years ago, we read a very moving article written by Bronnie Ware, an Australian palliative care nurse, about the "top regrets of people who were dying." Ware interviewed patients in palliative care units and nursing homes who were in their final days. The answers she compiled inspired us to really consider what it takes to live a more fulfilled and purposeful life, and one without regrets.

The No. 1 regret mentioned by seniors in the article was that they never pursued their dreams and aspirations. We have met a lot of people who were never brave enough to pursue their dreams and ended up settling for what others expected of them. These people are often haunted not by the decisions they made but by the opportunities they decided not to pursue.

We believe the only way to live a life without regret is to consistently exercise your risk muscle and be willing to learn from your failures when that muscle tears. We believe the greatest lessons you can learn are not from the deals you make money on, but from the ones you end up taking a loss. When you assess and reflect back on why you failed, you will often find the clues to what it takes to be successful.

Rule 8: Create a Culture That Believes in Personal Development

We have always been and always will be personal development junkies. If you turn us loose in a bookstore you may not find us for months. This never-ending curiosity and thirst for knowledge is a quality we see amongst many of our peers who earn in the high seven figures a year. It is second nature for some, and in others it is a quality that has to be developed and positively rewarded.

In our business, we have created a culture that rewards performance with further education. If we reach a goal we set, we will often reward our team members by sending them to personal development or educational seminars. We also spend a lot of time masterminding with each other about how to improve every area of our lives from our business to our health to our personal finances. This culture has helped us retain some of the most talented people in the real estate industry.

Rule 9: Find a Coach

Your real estate and business education will ultimately be your greatest asset. If you plan to be successful in this industry, we suggest you consistently dedicate at least five hours a week to your education and self-improvement. We also suggest you find a mentor who can coach and help you reach your financial goals.

In a recent survey of Fortune 500 CEOs, more than 70 percent said they had a business coach they worked with on a monthly basis. If you look at the most successful people in any industry, the majority are at the top of their field because they found someone who could mentor them early in their careers. Imagine what Michael Jordan's career and earnings would have looked like if he didn't have one of the best coaches in NBA history, Phil Jackson, working with him for the majority of his career.

The problem with just books, courses, and seminars is that they're not designed to fit all the different circumstances in your life. That's why coaching is so valuable. We coach a lot of investors and we create very specific plans for them to implement and leverage the systems we've already created, so they don't have to *reinvent the wheel*. Everyone has a unique set of circumstances, a different background and experience level, and a varied number of hours that they can work on a business.

Coaching is so valuable because it's tailored to your specific situation and your goals. You want to make half a million dollars? It's going be different from somebody who wants to make $200,000 versus somebody who only has ten hours a week and wants to make $75,000 a year. Your plan of attack is going to be different. That's why books, courses, and seminars can only take you so far. Coaching, on the other hand, can take you to where you really want to go.

Final Thoughts

As we close out this journey together, we want to remind you that you only have one life to live, so dare to dream. We sincerely hope this book has helped shift the way you think and the way in which you will approach building your real estate business. We hope this is a day you mark on your calendar the day when your business and your life took one giant leap forward.

Continue learning and implementing—and we have no doubt that you will prosper.

Finally, always remember to attack life eight days a week and enjoy the ride. ✤

For more information about how we can help you as a real estate investor go to: www.MasteryForInvestors.com.

AFTERWORD

Michael E. Gerber

For more than three decades, I've applied the E-Myth principles I've shared with you here to the successful development of thousands of small businesses throughout the world. Many have been real estate investment companies—from small companies to large corporations, with real estate investors specializing in markets all over the country.

Few rewards are greater than seeing these E-Myth principles improve the work and lives of so many people. Those rewards include seeing these changes:

- Lack of clarity—clarified
- Lack of organization—organized
- Lack of direction—shaped into a path that is clearly, lovingly, passionately pursued
- Lack of money or money poorly managed—money understood instead of coveted; created instead of chased; wisely spent or invested instead of squandered
- Lack of committed people—transformed into a cohesive community working in harmony toward a common goal; discovering one another and themselves in the process; all the while expanding their understanding, their know-how, their interest, their attention

After working with so many real estate investors, I know that a company can be much more than what most become. I also know that nothing is preventing you from making your company all that it can be. It takes only desire and the perseverance to see it through.

In this book—the next of its kind in the E-Myth Expert series—the E-Myth principles have been complemented and enriched by stories from real-life real estate investors, such as Than, who have put these principles to use in their company. Than and Paul had the desire and perseverance to achieve success beyond their wildest dreams. Now you, too, can join them their ranks.

I hope this book has helped you clear your vision and set your sights on a very bright future.

To your company and your life, good growing!

ABOUT THE AUTHOR

Michael E. Gerber

Michael E. Gerber is the international legend, author, and thought leader behind the E-Myth series of books, including *The E-Myth Revisited, E-Myth Mastery, The E-Myth Manager, The E-Myth Enterprise, The Most Successful Small Business in the World and Awakening the Entrepreneur Within.* Collectively, Mr. Gerber's books have sold millions of copies worldwide. Michael Gerber is the founder of Michael E. Gerber Companies, E-Myth Worldwide, The Dreaming Room™, and his newest venture, Design, Build, Launch & Grow™. Since 1977, Mr. Gerber's companies have served the business development needs of over 70,000 business clients in over 145 countries. Regarded by his avid followers as the thought leader of entrepreneurship worldwide, Mr. Gerber has been called by Inc. Magazine, "the world's #1 small business guru." A highly sought-after speaker and strategist, who has single handedly been accountable for the transformation of small business worldwide, Michael lives with his wife, Luz Delia, in Carlsbad, California.

ABOUT THE CO-AUTHORS

Than Merrill
Paul Esajian

Than Merrill and Paul Esajian are the co-founders of FortuneBuilders.com and CT Homes, along with Konrad Sopielnikow. In the past decade, they have bought and sold hundreds of properties, including everything from single-family to multifamily to commercial properties. They are also the stars in A&E's hit TV show *Flip This House*. Their expertise in running a successful real estate investment company is an invaluable resource for any aspiring real estate investor. Additionally, they coach hundreds of successful real estate investors in different markets around the country on how to build successful systems-dependent businesses. Than and Paul reside with their families in San Diego, California.

ABOUT THE SERIES

The E-Myth Expert series brings Michael E. Gerber's proven E-Myth philosophy to a wide variety of different professional business areas. The E-Myth, short for "Entrepreneurial Myth," is simple: Too many small businesses fail to grow because their leaders think like technicians, not entrepreneurs. Gerber's approach gives small enterprise leaders practical, proven methods that have already helped transform tens of thousands of businesses. Let the E-Myth Expert series boost your professional business today!

Books in the series include:

The E-Myth Attorney
The E-Myth Accountant
The E-Myth Optometrist
The E-Myth Chiropractor
The E-Myth Financial Advisor
The E-Myth Landscape Contractor
The E-Myth Architect
The E-Myth Real Estate Brokerage
The E-Myth Insurance Store
The E-Myth Dentist
The E-Myth Nutritionist
The E-Myth Bookkeeper
The E-Myth Real Estate Investor

Forthcoming books in the series include:

The E-Myth Veterinarian
. . . and 300 more industries and professions

Learn more at: www.michaelegerber.com/co-author

Have you created an E-Myth enterprise? Would you like to become a co-author of an E-Myth book in your industry? Go to www.michaelegerber.com/co-author.

THE MICHAEL E. GERBER
ENTREPRENEUR'S LIBRARY
It Keeps Growing . . .

Thank you for reading another E-Myth Vertical book.

Who do you know who is an expert in their industry?

Who has applied the E-Myth to the improvement of their
practice as Than Merrill and Paul Esajian have?

Who can add immense value to others in his or her industry
by sharing what he or she has learned?

Please share this book with that individual and share that individual with us.

We at Michael E. Gerber Companies are determined to transform the state
of small business and entrepreneurship worldwide. *You can help.*

To find out more, email us at Michael E. Gerber Partners, at
gerber@michaelegerber.com.

To find out how *YOU* can apply the E-Myth to *YOUR* practice,
contact us at gerber@michaelegerber.com.

Thank you for living your Dream, and changing the world.

Authors of Business Design

Michael E. Gerber, Co-Founder/Chairman
Michael E. Gerber Companies™
Creator of The E-Myth Evolution™
P.O. Box 131195, Carlsbad, CA 92013
760-752-1812 O • 760-752-9926 F
gerber@michaelegerber.com
www.michaelegerber.com

Join The Evolution^{SM}

Attend the Dreaming Room™ Trainings
www.michaelegerber.com/dreaming-room

Awaken the Entrepreneur Within You
www.michaelegerber.com/facilitator-training

Michael E. Gerber Partners
www.michaelegerber.com/are-you-the-one

Listen to the Michael E. Gerber Radio Show
www.blogtalkradio.com/michaelegerber

Watch the latest videos
www.youtube.com/michaelegerber

Connect on LinkedIn
www.linkedin.com/in/michaelegerber

Connect on Facebook
www.facebook.com/MichaelEGerberCo

Follow on Twitter
http://twitter.com/michaelegerber

CPSIA information can be obtained at www.ICGtesting.com
Printed in the USA
LVOW12*2328220615

443460LV00001B/1/P